DIVINE LEADERSHIP

Strategic Wisdom from the Bible

manoj sam & jay kumar

Published by

INDUS NETWORK

Fort Myers, Florida 33913

"Blessed are those who find wisdom, those who gain understanding, for she is more profitable than silver and yields better returns than gold."

Proverbs 3:13-14 (NIV)

Introduction

Divine Leadership" unveils a profound exploration of strategic leadership through the lens of biblical narratives, illustrating timeless principles that resonate across diverse arenas — business, community, and personal growth. In a world hungry for effective leadership, these stories offer not just inspiration but actionable insights that transcend time and culture.

Part I of the book, "Foundational Principles of Biblical Leadership," begins with Vision and Purpose, exemplified by Moses and Nehemiah. Moses, called to lead the Israelites out of Egypt, and Nehemiah, tasked with rebuilding Jerusalem's walls, epitomize visionary leadership. Their stories teach us the power of clarity in purpose and the transformative impact of rallying others towards a common goal.

Integrity and Character, crucial attributes in leadership, are vividly portrayed in the lives of Joseph and Daniel. Joseph's unwavering integrity in Egypt and Daniel's steadfastness in the face of persecution highlight the importance of moral courage and ethical leadership, essential for gaining trust and achieving long-term success.

Wisdom and Discernment, illustrated through Solomon's quest for wisdom and Paul's strategic decisions in ministry, underscore the necessity of informed decision-making. These leaders demonstrate how wisdom rooted in divine insight can navigate complexities and lead to sustainable outcomes.

Part II, "Leading through Challenges," explores narratives of Faith and Courage, Resilience and Perseverance, and Adaptability and Innovation. From David's daring confrontation with Goliath to Esther's bold stand for her people, these stories inspire leaders to confront adversity with faith, resilience, and innovative thinking.

Part III, "Building and Sustaining Effective Teams," delves into the dynamics of Servant Leadership, effective Communication and Collaboration, and Conflict Resolution leading to Unity. Jesus washing the disciples' feet and Nehemiah's strategic communication underscore the importance of humility and effective team building.

Part IV, "Legacy and Impact," examines Mentorship and Succession Planning, emphasizing the significance of investing in future leaders. From Moses mentoring Joshua to Paul guiding Timothy, these examples highlight the enduring impact of leadership development.

Ultimately, "Divine Leadership" is a roadmap for leaders seeking to integrate timeless biblical wisdom with modern leadership challenges. It equips readers not only with theoretical knowledge but practical strategies to lead with integrity, wisdom, and a servant's heart—leaving a legacy of positive influence and transformation in their respective spheres.

Contents

Part III
Building and Sustaining Effective Teams

Part IV
Legacy and Impact

11 Leaving a Lasting Legacy

Part I

Foundational Principles of Biblical Leadership

Chapter 1

Vision and Purpose

Vision and purpose are foundational to effective leadership, providing a framework that guides actions, inspires commitment, and drives organizational success.

A leader's vision is a clear, compelling picture of a desired future state or goal. It serves as a beacon, providing direction and aligning efforts towards a common objective. A well-defined vision not only outlines what needs to be achieved but also why it matters, inspiring enthusiasm and motivating individuals to contribute their best efforts. For example, visionary leaders like Steve Jobs at Apple articulated a future where technology seamlessly integrates with daily life, inspiring innovation and revolutionizing industries.

Purpose complements vision by infusing it with meaning and significance. It answers the question of why the envisioned future is worth pursuing, connecting it to deeper values and principles. Purpose-driven leaders are driven by a sense of mission that transcends personal ambition, focusing instead on making a positive impact on their organizations, communities, or even the world. For instance, leaders in social enterprises often derive purpose from addressing societal challenges or improving lives through their work.

Effective leadership combines vision and purpose to create alignment and motivation within teams. Leaders who communicate a compelling vision and connect it to a meaningful purpose inspire trust, loyalty, and engagement among their followers. They foster a culture where individuals understand their roles in achieving the collective vision and feel empowered to contribute creatively and enthusiastically.

Moreover, vision and purpose provide stability and guidance during times of uncertainty or change. They help leaders make decisions that are consistent with long-term goals and values, ensuring resilience and adaptability in dynamic environments.

1(a).

Moses and the Exodus

(Exodus 3 – 4)

In the rugged wilderness of Midian, where the sun beat down fiercely upon the desert land, Moses led the sheep of his father-in-law Jethro. His days were filled with the dusty routine of a shepherd, guiding his flock to find patches of greenery amidst the barren rocks.

One day, as the sheep grazed near the foot of Horeb, the mountain of God, Moses noticed a peculiar sight—a bush, ablaze with flames that danced without consuming its branches. Curiosity gripped him, and he approached the bush cautiously, drawn by its inexplicable fire.

As Moses drew near, a voice boomed from the midst of the flames, "Moses! Moses!"

Startled, Moses replied, "Here I am."

The voice spoke again, commanding him, "Do not come closer. Take off your sandals, for the place where you are standing is holy ground."

Moses obeyed, removing his sandals, feeling the rough earth beneath his feet. Trembling, he listened as the voice continued, "I am the God of your father, the God of Abraham, Isaac, and Jacob."

Overwhelmed by the presence of the divine, Moses hid his face, afraid to look upon the Lord.

"I have seen the suffering of my people in Egypt," the Lord declared solemnly. "I have heard their cries under the oppression of their taskmasters. I am aware of their pain, and I have come down to deliver them from bondage and lead them to a land flowing with milk and honey."

Moses, humbled and astonished, listened as the Lord continued, "Now go, for I am sending you to Pharaoh. You will bring my people, the Israelites, out of Egypt."

Fear and doubt seized Moses. "Who am I," he asked, "that I should go to Pharaoh and lead the Israelites out of Egypt?"

But the Lord reassured him, "I will be with you. And when you have brought the people out of Egypt, you will return to this very mountain and worship me."

Then Moses asked, "Suppose I go to the Israelites and tell them, 'The God of your ancestors has sent me to you,' and they ask me, 'What is his name?' What should I say to them?"

"I am who I am," the Lord replied. "This is what you are to say to the Israelites: 'I am has sent me to you.'"

With each word, Moses felt the weight of his calling settle upon him. He was to be the instrument of God's power and deliverance.

"Go and assemble the elders of Israel," the Lord instructed. "Tell them that the God of their fathers has appeared to you, and that I have seen their affliction in Egypt. They will listen to you."

But Moses, still uncertain of himself, pleaded, "What if they do not believe me?"

The Lord said, "What is that in your hand?"

"A staff," Moses replied.

"Throw it on the ground," the Lord commanded.

Moses obeyed, and the staff transformed into a slithering snake. Recoiling in fear, Moses watched as the Lord instructed him to seize it by the tail. In his grasp, the snake became a staff once more.

"If they do not believe this sign," the Lord said, "then take your hand and put it inside your cloak." When Moses withdrew his hand, it was stricken with leprosy. But upon returning it to his cloak, it was restored.

"And if they still do not believe you," the Lord added, "take water from the Nile and pour it on the ground. It will turn to blood."

Despite these signs, Moses felt inadequate. "Lord, I am not eloquent," he confessed. "I am slow of speech and tongue."

The Lord, patient yet firm, replied, "I will help you speak and teach you what to say."

But Moses persisted, "Please, send someone else."

At this, the Lord's patience wore thin. "What about your brother, Aaron?" he asked. "He is already on his way to meet you. He will speak for you to the people."

Reluctantly, Moses accepted the Lord's plan. He returned to his father-in-law, Jethro, seeking his blessing to leave for Egypt. With his wife and sons in tow, and the staff of God in his hand, Moses embarked on the journey back to the land of his birth.

Upon their arrival, the Lord reaffirmed his purpose to Moses: to perform wonders before Pharaoh, despite the hardness of his heart. The stage was set for the showdown between the God of Israel and the might of Egypt.

And so, with Aaron at his side and the promise of divine power, Moses stood ready to confront the ruler of Egypt and lead his people to freedom.

1. **Divine Presence and Holiness**: The encounter with the burning bush teaches about the holiness of God's presence. Moses had to remove his sandals because he stood on holy ground. This demonstrates reverence and acknowledgment of God's transcendence.

2. **God's Awareness and Concern**: God revealed Himself to Moses as the one who sees and hears the suffering of His people. This

underscores God's compassion and active involvement in human affairs, even in times of oppression and hardship.

3. **Divine Calling and Human Inadequacy**: Moses initially doubted his ability to fulfill God's call to confront Pharaoh and lead the Israelites out of Egypt. This highlights the tension between divine calling and human limitations. God's reassurance that He would be with Moses emphasizes reliance on divine strength rather than personal prowess.

4. **Names and Identity**: When Moses asked God His name, God replied, "I am who I am." This revelation of God's name signifies His eternal, unchanging nature and authority. It also emphasizes the importance of knowing and invoking God by His true identity.

5. **Signs and Wonders**: God equipped Moses with miraculous signs—the staff turning into a snake, Moses' hand becoming leprous and then healed, and water turning into blood. These signs authenticated Moses' divine commission and underscored God's power over natural elements.

6. **Divine Partnership**: Despite Moses' hesitation and insecurity, God provided Aaron as a partner to support and complement Moses in his mission. This illustrates God's willingness to work through human relationships and collaboration in fulfilling His purposes.

7. **Obedience and Trust**: Moses eventually obeyed God's call, demonstrating trust and faithfulness. His journey from doubt to obedience models how faith in God's promises can overcome human apprehension and reluctance.

8. **Preparation and Readiness**: Moses' preparation in the wilderness—his encounter with God, reception of signs, and

divine instructions—prepared him for the monumental task ahead. This highlights the importance of spiritual preparation and readiness for fulfilling God-given missions.

9. **Persistence in God's Plan**: Despite setbacks and Pharaoh's initial resistance, Moses persisted in carrying out God's plan. This perseverance in the face of adversity reflects the importance of steadfast faith and commitment to God's purposes.

10. **Leadership and Deliverance**: Moses' story ultimately illustrates God's faithfulness in using flawed individuals to lead His people to deliverance. It teaches about the transformative power of obedience, faith, and reliance on God in achieving liberation from bondage.

1(b).

Nehemiah rebuilding Jerusalem

(Nehemiah 1 – 2)

In the grand citadel of Susa, where the opulence of King Artaxerxes' court contrasted sharply with the concerns of distant lands, Nehemiah, a humble cupbearer, found himself troubled. It was the month of Kislev, the twentieth year of the king's reign, when Hanani, his brother, arrived from Judah with news that pierced Nehemiah's heart.

"Jerusalem," Hanani began solemnly, "lies in ruins. The walls are broken down, and its gates have been destroyed by fire. Those who survived the exile are in great trouble and disgrace."

Upon hearing this, Nehemiah was overcome with grief. He sat down, tears streaming down his face, mourning for days. He fasted and prayed fervently before the God of heaven, pouring out his heart in repentance and petition.

"Lord, God of heaven," Nehemiah prayed, his voice echoing in the quiet of his chamber, "you are great and awesome. You keep your covenant of love with those who love you and keep your commandments. Hear my prayer, day and night, for your people Israel. I confess the sins we have committed, including myself and my father's family. We have acted wickedly and have not obeyed your commands given through Moses."

Nehemiah continued, his voice trembling with emotion, "But you, Lord, promised that if we turned back to you and obeyed your commands, you would gather us from the farthest places and bring us to the place where you have chosen to dwell. Remember your promises, Lord. Your servants, whom you redeemed with your great power, are now in need of your mercy."

"Lord, hear the prayer of your servant," Nehemiah pleaded, "and of your servants who delight in revering your name. Grant me success today as I seek favor in the presence of the king."

For Nehemiah was not only a man of prayer but also the trusted cupbearer to King Artaxerxes himself.

Artaxerxes Sends Nehemiah to Jerusalem

Months later, in the month of Nisan of the same twentieth year, as Nehemiah served wine to the king, a rare sorrow weighed upon his countenance. The king, noticing his cupbearer's distress, inquired gently, "Why does your face look so sad? You are not ill; this can only be sadness of heart."

Fear gripped Nehemiah, but he gathered his courage and replied respectfully, "May the king live forever! Why should my face not be sad when the city where my ancestors are buried lies in ruins, and its gates have been destroyed by fire?"

"What is it that you request?" the king asked with genuine concern.

In that moment, Nehemiah turned his heart towards heaven. "May it please the king," he prayed silently, "to send me to Judah, to the city of my ancestors, that I may rebuild it."

Summoning his resolve, Nehemiah spoke, "If it pleases the king and if your servant has found favor in your sight, send me to Judah, to the city of my ancestors' tombs, that I may rebuild it."

The king, with the queen beside him, regarded Nehemiah thoughtfully. "How long will your journey take, and when will you return?" he inquired.

With gratitude to God filling his heart, Nehemiah answered, "With your blessing, O King, I will return within a set time."

Eager to assist Nehemiah in his mission, the king granted his request. Nehemiah then asked for letters to ensure safe passage through the lands beyond the Euphrates and for supplies to aid in the city's restoration. The king, moved by God's grace upon Nehemiah, readily provided all that was requested.

Thus empowered by the gracious hand of his God and the favor of the king, Nehemiah set out on his journey. He presented the king's letters to the governors of the Trans-Euphrates region and was accompanied by officers and cavalry as he embarked on his mission.

However, not all welcomed Nehemiah's mission with open arms.

When Sanballat the Horonite and Tobiah the Ammonite official heard of his intentions, they were deeply troubled. Their hearts were set against any prosperity for the people of Israel.

Undeterred, Nehemiah arrived in Jerusalem and began his work quietly, without fanfare. For three days, he surveyed the ruins of the city under cover of darkness, his heart heavy with the enormity of the task before him. He confided in no one about the divine purpose stirring within him.

After assessing the damage to the walls and gates, Nehemiah gathered the leaders of Jerusalem and shared with them his vision and the king's benevolence. He spoke of God's favor upon him and his mission.

"Come," Nehemiah urged them, "let us rebuild the walls of Jerusalem and end this disgrace."

Encouraged by Nehemiah's words and inspired by the gracious hand of God upon him, the people responded with resolve, "Let us start rebuilding."

Yet, amidst the determination and hope, opposition arose. Sanballat, Tobiah, and Geshem the Arab mocked and ridiculed the efforts of Nehemiah and the people. "What is this you are doing?" they scoffed. "Are you rebelling against the king?"

With unwavering faith, Nehemiah answered them boldly, "The God of heaven will give us success. We, his servants, will rebuild, but you have no share or claim in Jerusalem."

And so, Nehemiah's prayerful journey began—a journey marked by faith, courage, and the unyielding determination to restore honor to Jerusalem and its people, relying solely on the strength and guidance of the God of heaven.

1. **Response to Distress:** Nehemiah responded deeply to the news of Jerusalem's ruin, showing empathy and sorrow for his people's plight. His initial reaction teaches the importance of being sensitive to the suffering of others and taking action where possible.

2. **Power of Prayer:** Nehemiah's prayer was not just a formality but a heartfelt plea to God, acknowledging His greatness, confessing sins, and seeking His guidance and favor. This underscores the power of prayer in seeking divine intervention and guidance in times of need.

3. **Courage and Initiative:** Despite his position as a cupbearer, Nehemiah showed courage in approaching King Artaxerxes to request permission to rebuild Jerusalem. This demonstrates the importance of taking initiative and courageously pursuing what is right, even when faced with daunting challenges.

4. **Divine Providence:** Nehemiah recognized that his mission was not solely dependent on human efforts but on God's providence and favor. He trusted in God's promises and sought His guidance throughout his journey, illustrating faith in divine assistance.

5. **Leadership and Vision:** Nehemiah displayed effective leadership by casting a clear vision for rebuilding Jerusalem. He inspired the people, mobilized them to action, and dealt with opposition firmly. This highlights the importance of visionary leadership and

rallying others towards a common goal.

6. **Persistence in Adversity:** Despite facing opposition and ridicule from adversaries like Sanballat and Tobiah, Nehemiah remained steadfast in his faith and determination. His unwavering resolve teaches the value of persistence in the face of obstacles and challenges.

7. **Humility and Service:** Throughout his narrative, Nehemiah exhibited humility, acknowledging his role as a servant of both God and the king. His humility coupled with a servant-hearted approach to leadership serves as a model for effective leadership that prioritizes the needs of others.

Chapter 2

Integrity and Character

Integrity is the bedrock of effective leadership, serving as a crucial pillar that shapes trust, respect, and ethical behavior within organizations and communities. At its core, integrity entails consistency between one's words, actions, and principles, regardless of external pressures or temptations. In the realm of leadership, this steadfast adherence to moral and ethical standards is not merely desirable but essential for fostering a positive and productive environment.

Leaders with integrity inspire confidence and loyalty among their followers. By consistently demonstrating honesty, transparency, and accountability, they establish a culture where open communication thrives and ethical decision-making becomes the norm. This environment cultivates trust among team members, stakeholders, and the broader community, laying the groundwork for collaborative efforts and sustainable success.

Moreover, integrity in leadership extends beyond personal conduct; it influences organizational culture and shapes long-term outcomes. Leaders who prioritize integrity prioritize the greater good over personal gain, making decisions that benefit the organization and its stakeholders rather than serving selfish interests. This commitment to ethical behavior builds a reputation for reliability and fairness, attracting top talent and enhancing the organization's standing in the industry.

In times of crisis or uncertainty, integrity serves as a guiding light, helping leaders navigate complex challenges with integrity, resilience, and moral clarity. When leaders uphold high ethical standards, they inspire others to do the same, fostering a culture of integrity that permeates throughout the organization.

Integrity in leadership is not just a virtue but a strategic advantage. It builds credibility, enhances trust, and drives sustainable growth. Leaders who prioritize integrity set a powerful example, influencing positive change and leaving a legacy built on principles of honesty, fairness, and ethical responsibility.

2(a).

Joseph's integrity in Egypt

(Genesis 39-41)

In the land of Egypt, where the sands whispered ancient tales of Pharaohs and gods, Joseph found himself a stranger, sold into servitude by his own brothers' hands. Yet, the divine hand of providence guided his path, even in the house of Potiphar, captain of Pharaoh's guard.

From the moment Joseph entered Potiphar's household, it was evident that the Lord's favor rested upon him. His diligence and wisdom were soon recognized, and Potiphar entrusted him with the care of his entire estate. The blessings of Joseph's stewardship overflowed, bringing prosperity to all that Potiphar possessed, be it in the fields or within the walls of his grand house.

But amidst this success, Joseph faced a trial that tested his integrity to its core. Potiphar's wife, a woman of beauty and desire, cast her eyes upon Joseph. Day after day, she tempted him with her words, beckoning him to lie with her. Yet Joseph, a man of steadfast faith and honor, refused her advances, declaring, "How then could I do such a wicked thing and sin against God?"

Undeterred by his rejection, Potiphar's wife seized an opportunity when they were alone in the house. She grasped his cloak, demanding once more that he come to her. In a desperate bid to escape her grasp and the allure of sin, Joseph fled, leaving his cloak in her hands as evidence of her deceit.

Enraged and humiliated, Potiphar's wife concocted a false accusation, claiming Joseph had dishonored her. She showed his cloak to her servants, spinning a tale of Joseph's betrayal. When Potiphar returned, he listened to his wife's fabricated story and, consumed by anger, cast Joseph into the darkness of the prison.

Yet, even in the depths of confinement, the Lord did not abandon Joseph. His presence was a beacon of hope in the gloom, and Joseph soon found favor with the prison warden. Entrusted with authority over his fellow prisoners, Joseph bore his burden with grace, demonstrating his unwavering faith in the Almighty.

Through Joseph's unwavering integrity and divine guidance, even the darkest hour became a testament to the power of faith and righteousness. His story, from the heights of Potiphar's household to the depths of the prison, would echo through generations, a testament to the triumph of integrity and the enduring strength found in God's providence.

1. **Integrity in the Face of Temptation**: Joseph's steadfast refusal to compromise his moral principles, despite persistent advances from Potiphar's wife, underscores the importance of integrity. He prioritized faithfulness to God over fleeting desires, demonstrating resilience against moral and ethical challenges.

2. **Resilience in Adversity**: Despite being unjustly accused and imprisoned, Joseph did not lose faith. His ability to endure hardship with dignity and grace reveals resilience born from his unwavering trust in divine providence. This resilience enabled him to rise above circumstances and maintain hope.

3. **Divine Providence and Guidance**: Throughout Joseph's journey, God's presence was evident, guiding him from slavery to positions of authority. His story illustrates that faithfulness and trust in God's plan can lead to unexpected blessings and opportunities, even in the midst of adversity.

4. **Consequences of False Accusations**: Joseph's experience with Potiphar's wife highlights the repercussions of false accusations and the importance of seeking truth before passing judgment. His unjust punishment serves as a reminder of the need for fairness and integrity in interpersonal relationships and justice systems.

5. **Leadership through Service**: Even in prison, Joseph's leadership qualities shone through as he was entrusted with responsibilities and authority. His willingness to serve others with compassion and diligence, despite his own predicament, exemplifies true leadership rooted in humility and empathy.

6. **Legacy of Faith and Righteousness**: Joseph's life journey—from slavery to a position of power—leaves a legacy of faithfulness, righteousness, and forgiveness. His story inspires generations to uphold moral values, trust in God's plan, and persevere through adversity with grace and humility.

2(b).

Daniel In the Lion's Den

(Daniel 6)

In the grand city of Babylon, where the Euphrates River flowed lazily past towering palaces and bustling markets, King Darius reigned with authority and wisdom. He had appointed Daniel, a man of exceptional integrity and wisdom, as one of the three administrators over the vast kingdom. Daniel's reputation soared as he distinguished himself among the satraps and administrators, earning the king's admiration.

But envy simmered among Daniel's peers. They watched with jealousy as Daniel's star rose higher, his every decision marked by fairness and honesty. No hint of corruption tainted his service to the kingdom.

Frustrated by their inability to find fault with Daniel's governance, the administrators and satraps devised a malicious plan. Gathering together, they approached King Darius with flattering words, proposing an unprecedented edict: for thirty days, no one in the kingdom should pray to any god or man except the king himself, under the penalty of being cast into the lions' den.

In his pride and unaware of their true intentions, King Darius agreed, issuing the decree with the seal of the Medes and Persians, ensuring its irrevocability. The kingdom buzzed with the news of the decree, spreading fear among those who worshipped other gods and prompting whispers of discontent.

Daniel, however, remained steadfast in his faith. From his chamber with windows open toward Jerusalem, he continued his daily practice of prayer, kneeling before God three times a day, offering thanks and seeking guidance just as he had always done.

The jealous conspirators, ever watchful, soon caught Daniel in prayer. They wasted no time in reporting him to King Darius, reminding him of the decree he had signed. Distressed and deeply troubled, Darius understood the implications. He cherished Daniel's wisdom and loyalty, knowing that his advisors sought not justice but to eliminate a righteous man.

Reluctantly, bound by the unchangeable law he had invoked, Darius ordered Daniel brought before him. With a heavy heart, he commanded that Daniel be cast into the den of hungry lions. As Daniel stood at the brink, facing the roaring beasts below, Darius spoke with a tremor in his voice, "May your God, whom you serve continually, rescue you!"

The den was sealed with a heavy stone and the king's signet, marking Daniel's fate. Darius returned to his palace, tormented by thoughts of Daniel's plight. Throughout the night, he neither ate nor sought entertainment, wrestling with the consequences of his decree and praying silently for Daniel's deliverance.

At the first light of dawn, before the city stirred awake, Darius rushed to the den. His heart pounded with fear and hope as he called out, "Daniel, servant of the living God, has your God, whom you serve continually, been able to rescue you from the lions?"

A voice, clear and unwavering, echoed from within the darkness, "May the king live forever! My God sent his angel, and he shut the mouths of the lions. They have not harmed me, because I was found innocent in his sight. Nor have I ever done any wrong before you, Your Majesty."

Relief flooded Darius's heart as he ordered the stone lifted. Daniel emerged unscathed, untouched by the jaws of the fierce lions. His faith had been his shield, and God had proven faithful in protecting His servant.

Overcome with joy and gratitude, Darius ordered Daniel lifted from the den. Not a scratch marked his body, a testament to the power of unwavering faith. In a swift turn of justice, the conspirators who had schemed against Daniel were brought before the king. With grim resolve, Darius sentenced them and their families to face the lions' den, where justice met swift and final retribution.

Moved by the miraculous deliverance of Daniel and the power of his God, Darius proclaimed a decree throughout his kingdom and beyond. His voice carried across borders and languages, declaring the greatness of the God of Daniel, the living God who rescues and saves.

1. **Uncompromising Faith**: Daniel's unwavering commitment to his faith is central to the story. Despite knowing the consequences, he continued to pray faithfully to God, refusing to compromise his beliefs even under threat of death. This teaches us the importance of standing firm in our convictions and trusting in God's faithfulness, regardless of external pressures or risks.

2. **Integrity and Character**: Daniel's impeccable integrity and character earned him favor and respect, even among those who sought his downfall. His commitment to honesty and fairness in all his dealings set him apart and ultimately led to his vindication. This underscores the timeless principle that integrity is foundational to earning trust and honor.

3. **Divine Protection and Deliverance**: The miraculous intervention of God, who shut the mouths of the lions and preserved Daniel unharmed, highlights the power of divine protection for those who trust in Him. It serves as a powerful reminder that God is sovereign over all circumstances and can deliver His faithful servants from any peril.

4. **Justice and Consequences**: The swift justice meted out to Daniel's accusers underscores the principle that falsehood and malice ultimately lead to their own downfall. Darius's decision to punish the conspirators and their families with the same fate they intended for Daniel illustrates the biblical concept of reaping what one sows.

5. **Proclamation of God's Greatness**: King Darius's proclamation of the greatness of Daniel's God to all nations and peoples reflects

the impact of witnessing God's miraculous power. It echoes the call to bear witness to God's faithfulness and sovereignty in our lives, spreading His glory and inspiring faith in others.

Chapter 3

Wisdom and Discernment

Wisdom and discernment are two qualities deeply intertwined yet distinct in their application and essence. Together, they form a powerful combination that shapes decision-making, understanding, and ultimately, the course of our lives.

Wisdom, often regarded as the culmination of knowledge and experience, transcends mere accumulation of facts. It encompasses the ability to apply understanding in a way that promotes sound judgment and a deeper comprehension of life's complexities. Wisdom is cultivated through learning from mistakes, reflecting on experiences, and gaining insights that go beyond the surface level of knowledge. It involves not just knowing what to do, but understanding why it should be done and the potential consequences of actions.

Discernment, on the other hand, complements wisdom by focusing on the ability to perceive and distinguish between different elements or perspectives. It involves keen insight, intuition, and a sharp awareness of nuances that may not be immediately apparent. Discernment allows individuals to navigate through situations with clarity, identifying truth from falsehood, genuine from superficial, and beneficial from harmful.

Together, wisdom and discernment form a dynamic duo in decision-making. Wisdom provides the foundational knowledge and principles, while discernment acts as the lens through which this wisdom is applied to specific circumstances. For example, a wise person may have learned over years of experience how to manage finances prudently. However, discernment would enable them to recognize when a seemingly lucrative investment opportunity carries too much risk.

In personal growth and spiritual development, wisdom and discernment are invaluable. They help individuals make choices aligned with their values, navigate ethical dilemmas, and foster harmonious relationships. Cultivating these qualities involves ongoing introspection, learning from mentors and peers, and honing the ability to listen not only to others but also to one's own inner voice.

3.(a).

Solomon's Request for Wisdom

(1 Kings 3)

King Solomon stood in the grand hall of his palace, surrounded by his courtiers and officials, the weight of his kingdom resting heavily upon his shoulders. The city of Jerusalem bustled outside the palace walls, its people watching with reverence and curiosity as their wise young king prepared to dispense justice.

On this particular day, two women approached the throne, their faces marked by sorrow and desperation. They knelt before Solomon, their voices trembling as they presented their case.

"Pardon me, my lord," began the first woman, her eyes pleading. "This woman and I live in the same house. Recently, I gave birth to a son. Three days later, she also bore a son. Last night, her son died, and she switched our babies while I slept."

The second woman, her voice just as anguished, countered

vehemently, "No! The living child is mine; the dead one is hers."

The courtroom buzzed with tension as Solomon listened intently, his discerning gaze shifting from one woman to the other. He knew that the truth often hid in the depths of human emotion.

"Bring me a sword," Solomon commanded with authority, his voice cutting through the air.

A guard swiftly brought the king a gleaming sword, its blade reflecting the sunlight streaming through the palace windows. The courtroom held its breath as Solomon issued his fateful decree.

"Cut the living child in two and give half to one woman and half to the other."

Gasps echoed through the hall as the women's faces paled in horror. The first woman, overcome with maternal love, cried out in desperation, "Please, my lord, give her the living baby! Don't kill him!"

But the second woman, unmoved, coldly declared, "Neither I nor you shall have him. Cut him in two!"

Solomon observed their reactions keenly, his heart heavy with the weight of his decision. In that moment, wisdom granted by the divine guided his hand. "Give the living baby to the first woman. Do not kill him; she is his mother."

The courtroom erupted into murmurs of awe and admiration. Word spread swiftly through the streets of Jerusalem: Solomon, blessed by God with wisdom beyond measure, had delivered a just and merciful judgment.

From that day onward, Solomon's reputation as a wise and just ruler spread far and wide. People traveled from distant lands to witness his wisdom firsthand, and all who stood before him marveled at the discernment with which he governed. Solomon's prayer for wisdom had been granted abundantly, ensuring that his reign would be remembered throughout history as a testament to divine guidance and the power of righteous judgment.

1. **Wisdom in Judgment**: Solomon's ability to discern the truth from conflicting claims illustrates the importance of wisdom in making fair and just decisions. His wisdom goes beyond mere intellect; it involves understanding human nature and motivations.
2. **Justice and Compassion**: Solomon's judgment demonstrates the balance between justice and compassion. While he initially proposes a drastic measure to reveal the true mother, he ultimately shows compassion by sparing the child's life and giving him to the rightful mother.
3. **Depth of Human Emotion**: The story highlights how emotions can obscure or reveal the truth. Solomon recognizes that genuine maternal love prompts selflessness, whereas selfish motives are driven by indifference or malice.
4. **Divine Guidance**: Solomon attributes his wisdom to divine guidance. This suggests a belief in seeking wisdom beyond one's own abilities, relying on spiritual or moral principles to navigate complex situations.
5. **Leadership and Reputation**: Solomon's wise judgment enhances his reputation as a leader. Leaders who exhibit wisdom and fairness attract respect and admiration, not only locally but also

from distant lands, symbolizing the enduring impact of just governance.

6. **Historical Legacy**: The story underscores how acts of wisdom and justice can shape historical legacy. Solomon's reign is remembered as a testament to divine wisdom and the power of righteous judgment, influencing generations beyond his own time.

3(b).

The Discernment of The Apostle Paul

(Acts 16:6-10)

Paul and his companions, weary yet steadfast in their mission, journeyed through the rugged terrain of Phrygia and Galatia. The Holy Spirit, their constant guide, directed their steps, restraining them from proclaiming the gospel in the province of Asia. Though the message burned within them, they yielded to the divine leading.

As they approached the border of Mysia, anticipation filled their hearts. Surely here, in Bithynia beyond, they would share the good news. Yet, the Spirit of Jesus intervened once more, closing the doors they sought to enter. Perplexed but obedient, they continued their journey, moving down toward the coastal city of Troas.

It was in Troas, amid the restless night, that Paul received a vision. In the dim hours, as the world slept, a figure emerged in his dreams—a man from Macedonia, earnestly pleading, "Come over to Macedonia and help us."

Startled yet stirred with purpose, Paul awoke with a deep conviction. He gathered his companions, recounting the vision that had pierced the veil of sleep. Together, they discerned the hand of God beckoning them across the Aegean Sea to the land of Macedonia.

With the dawn, preparations began swiftly. Supplies were gathered, prayers ascended, and hearts were fortified with the certainty that they carried a divine commission. The call to Macedonia resonated within them as a summons from heaven itself—a mandate to bring the gospel to those who awaited salvation.

In Troas, the bustling port city, they made ready to depart. The sails of a ship, bound for Neapolis, caught the morning breeze. Paul and his companions embarked, leaving behind the familiar shores of Asia Minor for the unknown shores of Europe.

As the ship cut through the waters, Paul reflected on the unfolding of divine providence. Each closed door, every redirection, had paved the way to this pivotal moment. The vision of the Macedonian man remained vivid in his mind—a reminder that God's plans often unfold through unexpected paths and unforeseen encounters.

The voyage across the Aegean was marked by anticipation and prayerful reflection. They sailed onward, propelled by the winds of God's Spirit and guided by the vision that had set their course. Ahead lay Macedonia, a land rich in history and culture, yet hungry for the eternal truths they carried.

As the ship approached the harbor of Neapolis, the gateway to Macedonia, Paul's heart quickened with anticipation. The journey had been long, the challenges many, but their resolve remained steadfast. They disembarked onto Macedonian soil, ready to fulfill their divine calling—to preach the gospel, to bring hope, and to ignite faith in the hearts of those who awaited them.

In that moment, Paul knew with unwavering certainty that God's hand had orchestrated their path. The vision of the Macedonian man had not been a mere dream, but a prophetic glimpse into the unfolding of God's redemptive plan. With grateful hearts and eager spirits, they set foot on Macedonian soil, ready to embark on the next chapter of their journey—the proclamation of salvation to a new land and a new people.

1. **Divine Guidance and Obedience**: Paul and his companions exemplify the importance of yielding to divine guidance. Despite their eagerness to spread the gospel in certain regions, they obediently followed the leading of the Holy Spirit and the Spirit of Jesus, even when it meant redirecting their plans.

2. **Discernment of God's Will**: The vision of the Macedonian man underscored the necessity of discerning God's will amidst uncertainties and closed doors. Paul's immediate response to the vision demonstrates sensitivity to divine direction and a readiness to act upon it.

3. **Flexibility in Ministry**: The journey through Phrygia, Galatia, and the attempt to enter Bithynia highlight the need for flexibility in ministry. God's plans often unfold differently than expected, requiring openness to new directions and readiness to adapt to unforeseen circumstances.

4. **Preparation and Readiness**: Upon receiving the vision, Paul and his companions swiftly prepared for the journey to Macedonia. This emphasizes the importance of readiness and preparation when responding to God's call, ensuring that they were equipped both spiritually and practically for the mission ahead.

5. **Trust in God's Providence**: Reflecting on their journey, Paul recognized God's providential guidance in every closed door and redirection. This teaches the lesson of trusting in God's sovereignty and providence, knowing that He orchestrates circumstances for His divine purposes.

6. **Mission to the Unreached**: The call to Macedonia represents a broader lesson in mission—to bring the gospel to those who have not yet heard. Paul's obedience to cross into Europe symbolizes the universal scope of God's redemptive plan and the urgency of reaching out to all nations and peoples.

7. **Courage and Perseverance**: The journey to Macedonia was not without challenges, yet Paul and his companions demonstrated courage and perseverance. This teaches the lesson of enduring faithfulness in fulfilling God's calling, despite obstacles and uncertainties along the way.

Part II

Leading through Challenges

Chapter 4

Faith and Courage

In the realm of leadership, navigating the complexities of uncertainty and inspiring others to move forward often hinges on two indispensable qualities: faith and courage. These attributes are not merely personal virtues but essential tools that enable leaders to surmount obstacles, drive change, and foster resilience in their teams and organizations.

Faith in this context transcends religious connotations to embody a profound belief in oneself, in others, and in the vision or mission that propels the leader forward. It is the unwavering confidence that despite challenges and setbacks, a brighter future awaits through perseverance and commitment. Leaders with faith exude optimism and clarity, instilling a sense of purpose that galvanizes their teams even during tumultuous times. This faith serves as a guiding light, illuminating the path ahead when the way forward seems obscured by doubt or fear.

Courage, on the other hand, complements faith by empowering leaders to take decisive action in the face of adversity. It is the audacity to confront risks, make tough decisions, and embrace vulnerability when necessary. Courageous leaders acknowledge uncertainty but refuse to be paralyzed by it; instead, they forge ahead with determination and integrity. They inspire trust and respect by embodying authenticity and resilience, demonstrating that setbacks are not defeats but opportunities for growth and innovation.

Together, faith and courage form a symbiotic relationship that amplifies a leader's effectiveness. Faith provides the foundation of belief and hope, while courage supplies the strength and fortitude to act decisively upon that belief. This combination enables leaders to envision possibilities beyond the immediate challenges, fostering an environment where creativity flourishes, and solutions emerge from adversity.

4(a).

David and Goliath

(1 Samuel 17)

David stood amidst the murmurs and trembling hearts of his fellow Israelites, the distant silhouette of Goliath casting a long shadow over the valley. The towering Philistine champion, clad in armor that gleamed in the morning sun, had thrown down his challenge day after day. His voice thundered across the valley, mocking the armies of Israel, challenging them to send forth a champion to face him in single combat.

David, though just a youth, burned with a fierce determination that defied his age. As he approached the camp, the atmosphere was heavy with fear and uncertainty. The seasoned warriors whispered cautiously, warning him of the peril that awaited anyone who dared confront Goliath.

Ignoring their apprehension, David sought out his brothers among the ranks. His eyes fixed on the colossal figure of Goliath pacing confidently on the Philistine side. David's heart swelled not with fear, but with a steadfast faith in the God of Israel. His hands trembled not with doubt, but with the anticipation of the battle to come.

When Saul summoned him, David stepped forward, resolute. Saul, in his armor, offered David his own gear, but the boy declined. Instead, he chose his shepherd's staff and a sling, and with five smooth stones gathered from a nearby brook, he prepared for battle.

As David approached the valley floor, the ground beneath his feet seemed to tremble with the weight of history about to unfold. Goliath's taunts grew louder, his voice echoing across the valley. The giant's shield bearer walked before him, a shadowy figure anticipating an easy victory over this boy who dared challenge him.

With each step, David's resolve strengthened. He spoke not of his own might, but of the power of the God he served—the living God of Israel who would deliver the Philistine into his hands.

Goliath, upon seeing David, scoffed at the sight of this young adversary. He cursed and threatened, but David remained undeterred. With a steady hand and a focused eye, he placed a stone in his sling and let it fly.

The stone struck true, finding its mark on Goliath's forehead. The giant stumbled, then fell heavily to the ground. The earth seemed to shake as the Philistine champion met his end, his mighty form now lifeless before the eyes of both armies.

Victory surged through the ranks of Israel as they realized the impossible had been achieved through the faith and courage of one young shepherd boy. The Philistines, witnessing their champion's defeat, fled in terror. The tide of battle turned, and the Israelites pursued their enemies, reclaiming their honor and plundering the Philistine camp.

David, holding Goliath's severed head aloft, became a symbol of faith and courage that resonated throughout the land. Saul, awestruck by this unexpected heroism, sought to learn more of the young man who had brought such glory to Israel.

Thus, on that day in the Valley of Elah, a shepherd boy named David emerged not only as a warrior but as a leader—anointed by destiny and driven by unwavering faith in the God who makes all things possible.

1. **Courage in the Face of Adversity**: David's courage in confronting Goliath, a formidable foe, teaches us the importance of facing our fears head-on. Despite the overwhelming odds and the fear instilled in his fellow Israelites, David stood firm, showing that courage is not the absence of fear but the ability to act despite it.

2. **Faith and Trust in God**: David's unwavering faith in God's protection and guidance is a central theme. His declaration that the battle belongs to the Lord underscores the power of faith in overcoming seemingly insurmountable challenges. It teaches us that with faith, even the most daunting obstacles can be overcome.

3. **Preparation and Utilization of Strengths**: David's choice of simple weapons—a sling and stones—demonstrates the importance of knowing and utilizing one's strengths. He rejected Saul's armor, opting instead for what he was familiar with and skilled at using. This teaches us the value of preparation and leveraging our unique abilities in tackling challenges.

4. **Leadership Through Initiative**: David's initiative to step forward and offer himself as a champion when others hesitated shows leadership in action. True leaders do not wait for others to act but take initiative, inspire others through their actions, and set an example of courage and conviction.

5. **Humility and Defiance of Expectations**: Despite his youth and humble origins as a shepherd, David defied expectations and achieved greatness. His humility in the face of criticism from his brothers and King Saul, and his unwavering resolve, serve as a reminder that greatness often comes from unexpected places.

6. **Symbolism of Triumph Over Oppression**: David's victory over Goliath symbolizes the triumph of the righteous over oppression and tyranny. It inspires hope and perseverance in the face of injustice, showing that even the smallest and seemingly weakest can bring about significant change.

7. **Legacy of Inspiration**: David's triumph resonated beyond the battlefield, inspiring generations with its tale of courage, faith, and leadership. It reminds us that our actions can have far-reaching consequences, influencing others positively and leaving a lasting legacy of hope and determination.

4(b).

Esther's Courage to Save Her People

(Esther 4-7)

Mordecai, a man of wisdom and faith, paced the streets of Susa with a heavy heart. The edict of destruction against the Jews had cast a pall of mourning over the city. Sackcloth and ashes adorned the grieving, their cries rising in lamentation.

Esther, nestled within the palace walls, learned of Mordecai's anguish through her attendants. She, too, felt the weight of her people's plight. With urgency, she dispatched Hathak, a trusted eunuch, to ascertain the cause of Mordecai's distress.

Hathak found Mordecai at the king's gate, his visage lined with sorrow. Mordecai, in solemn tones, recounted the grim reality facing their people—the decree that spelled annihilation. He showed Hathak the damning edict sealed by the king's command, detailing Haman's sinister plot and the bounty promised for the destruction of the Jews.

Hathak hastened back to Esther, bearing Mordecai's plea. Esther, shaken to her core, grappled with the enormity of the task ahead. She knew well the risks of approaching King Xerxes unbidden—death awaited any who dared enter his presence without his summons. Fear gripped her heart, but Mordecai's words echoed with profound clarity.

In response to Hathak's report, Esther conveyed her predicament to Mordecai through her attendants. Mordecai's reply cut through her hesitation, reminding her that her position as queen did not exempt her from the fate of her people. He spoke of providence and destiny, suggesting that perhaps her rise to queenship had prepared her precisely for this pivotal moment.

Esther, resolute in her decision, sent word back to Mordecai. She called upon all Jews in Susa to fast and pray for three days and nights, seeking divine guidance and strength. Esther and her attendants would join them in fasting, preparing themselves spiritually for what lay ahead.

Mordecai, faithful to Esther's instructions, organized the fast among the Jews of Susa. Three days of solemn prayer ensued, uniting their hearts in petition to the God of their ancestors.

At the end of the appointed time, Esther adorned herself in royal attire—a symbol of her readiness to face the king. With measured steps, she entered the inner court of the palace, where King Xerxes held court.

The sight of Queen Esther, radiant yet solemn, caught the king's attention. He extended the golden scepter—a sign of his favor—

towards her, granting her permission to approach.

Esther, gathering her courage, made her request known to the king. She invited him and Haman to a banquet she had prepared, delaying her petition until the following day.

The king, pleased by Esther's presence and intrigued by her request, agreed eagerly. He summoned Haman, and together they attended the banquet Esther had meticulously orchestrated.

As they indulged in wine and revelry, the king pressed Esther again for her petition. Esther, choosing her words carefully, revealed her plea: to spare her people, the Jews, from the impending doom decreed by Haman.

Meanwhile, Haman, elated by his status and the king's favor, departed the banquet in high spirits. His joy, however, quickly soured when he encountered Mordecai at the palace gate—still unmoved, still defiant.

Returning home, Haman boasted to his wife and friends of his glory and wealth. Yet, Mordecai's refusal to bow gnawed at him, overshadowing his pride.

Driven by rage and vengeance, Haman sought solace in his closest confidants. They counseled him to erect a gallows fifty cubits high, planning Mordecai's execution come morning.

That night, sleep eluded King Xerxes. In a twist of fate orchestrated by divine providence, he called for the chronicles of his reign to be read aloud. Among the records, the tale of Mordecai's foiling of an assassination plot unfolded—his loyalty and service to the king unrecognized and unrewarded.

As dawn broke, Haman arrived at the palace, intent on securing Mordecai's demise. Instead, he found himself summoned into the king's presence.

King Xerxes, seeking counsel, asked Haman how best to honor a man deserving of recognition. Blinded by arrogance, Haman suggested an elaborate ceremony fit for a king.

The king, with a wry smile, instructed Haman to bestow such honors upon Mordecai—the very man who had remained resolute in his defiance.

Haman, compelled by royal decree, obeyed begrudgingly. He draped Mordecai in regal attire, seated him on a majestic steed, and paraded him through the streets of Susa—an unwitting participant in his own humiliation.

Mordecai returned to the king's gate, now garlanded with honor and prestige, while Haman, his pride shattered, fled in disgrace to his home.

There, his wife and advisors, recognizing the gravity of his situation, warned him of impending ruin. The tables had turned, and Haman's downfall seemed inevitable.

Before Haman could contemplate his next move, the king's eunuchs arrived to escort him to Esther's second banquet—a banquet that would mark the beginning of the end for the proud Haman.

1. **Courage in the Face of Adversity**: Esther exemplifies courage by risking her life to approach King Xerxes without a summons. Despite the dangers, she chooses to act for the greater good of her people, demonstrating that courage often requires personal sacrifice.

2. **The Power of Prayer and Fasting**: Mordecai and Esther call for a period of fasting and prayer among the Jews in Susa. This spiritual discipline not only unites the community but also prepares Esther mentally and emotionally for her daunting task. It underscores the importance of seeking divine guidance in times of crisis.

3. **Leadership and Responsibility**: Mordecai challenges Esther to recognize her position of influence and responsibility. He reminds her that leadership demands action, especially when one's own people are in peril. Esther's journey from initial hesitation to decisive action highlights the responsibilities that come with leadership.

4. **Divine Providence and Timing**: The story portrays a belief in divine providence—that Esther's rise to queenship and Mordecai's position at the king's gate were not mere coincidence but part of a larger plan to save their people. It underscores the idea that sometimes events unfold in ways beyond human comprehension or control.

5. **Humility and Justice**: Haman's downfall serves as a cautionary tale about pride and injustice. His arrogance blinds him to the consequences of his actions, leading to his eventual disgrace. Conversely, Mordecai's humility and steadfastness in the face of adversity are rewarded with honor and recognition.

6. **Standing Against Injustice**: The narrative encourages individuals to stand against injustice, even at great personal risk. Mordecai and Esther's actions inspire others to resist tyranny and advocate for justice, showing that one person's courage can spark change for an entire community.

7. **The Role of Providence in History**: The unfolding events underscore a belief in the guiding hand of providence in human history. From Esther's bold petition to the king to Haman's unintended role in honoring Mordecai, the story illustrates how circumstances can align to bring about justice and redemption.

Chapter 5

Resilience and Perseverance

Resilience and perseverance are twin virtues that define our ability to navigate life's challenges with strength and determination. Resilience, often described as the capacity to bounce back from adversity, goes hand in hand with perseverance, the steadfastness in pursuing goals despite difficulties or delays.

At its core, resilience is about adapting to setbacks, learning from failures, and finding inner strength to overcome obstacles. It's not merely about enduring hardships passively but actively seeking ways to grow and thrive in spite of them. Resilient individuals demonstrate a mindset that views setbacks as temporary and surmountable, rather than insurmountable barriers.

Perseverance complements resilience by embodying the commitment and tenacity needed to stay the course in pursuit of long-term goals. It involves grit, the willingness to persist even when faced with challenges, setbacks, or criticism. Perseverance requires a clear sense of purpose and a willingness to endure discomfort or uncertainty along the journey towards achievement.

Together, resilience and perseverance form a powerful combination that propels individuals forward in the face of adversity. They empower us to face life's trials with courage and optimism, knowing that every setback is an opportunity for growth and every challenge a chance to prove our resilience.

In practice, developing resilience and perseverance involves cultivating self-awareness, fostering a positive outlook, and nurturing a support network of friends, family, or mentors. It requires embracing change, adapting to new circumstances, and learning from setbacks rather than allowing them to define us.

Ultimately, resilience and perseverance are not just attributes but skills that can be cultivated and strengthened over time. They enable us to weather life's storms with grace, emerge stronger on the other side, and inspire others with our ability to overcome adversity.

5(a).

Job's Endurance Through Suffering

(Book of Job)

In the land of Uz, there lived a man named Job. He was esteemed by all who knew him, not only for his wealth and prosperity but also for his integrity and righteousness. Job was a man of deep faith, devout in his worship of the Almighty, and committed to a life of virtue.

One day, as the sun cast its golden rays upon the fields of Uz, a heavenly council gathered before the presence of the Lord. Among them was Satan, the adversary, who roamed the earth seeking whom he could challenge. The Lord, knowing Job's faithfulness, spoke to Satan, "Have you considered my servant Job? There is no one like him on earth, a blameless and upright man who fears God and shuns evil."

Satan, with a hint of skepticism in his voice, replied, "Does Job fear God for nothing? Have you not placed a hedge around him and his household, blessing the work of his hands? But stretch out your hand and strike everything he has, and he will surely curse you to your face."

The Lord, confident in Job's faith, granted permission to Satan to test Job's integrity, with the condition that he spare Job's life. And so, in a swift whirlwind of calamity, messengers arrived one after another, bearing news of devastation.

First came a messenger who reported, "The Sabeans attacked and stole your oxen and donkeys, and they killed your servants with the sword. I alone have escaped to tell you."

Before Job could comprehend the first blow, another messenger arrived, panting and weary, "Fire fell from the heavens and burned up your sheep and the servants tending them. I alone have escaped to tell you."

As if in relentless succession, a third messenger appeared, his face marked with anguish, "The Chaldeans formed three raiding parties and swept down on your camels. They took them away, and they killed your servants with the sword. I alone have escaped to tell you."

Job's heart sank with each successive report, yet he fell to the ground and worshiped, saying, "Naked I came from my mother's womb, and naked I will depart. The Lord gave and the Lord has taken away; may the name of the Lord be praised."

Satan, undeterred by Job's steadfastness, beseeched the Lord once more, "Skin for skin! A man will give all he has for his own life. But stretch out your hand and strike his flesh and bones, and he will surely curse you to your face."

The Lord granted Satan permission once again, but instructed him not to take Job's life. And so, with a ferocity that shook Job to his core, painful boils erupted over his entire body. Job, now sitting in ashes, took a piece of broken pottery and scraped himself with it as he sat among the ashes.

His wife, seeing the depths of his affliction, could bear it no longer. "Are you still maintaining your integrity? Curse God and die!" she exclaimed in anguish.

But Job, his spirit undiminished despite the agony, replied with unwavering faith, "You are talking like a foolish woman. Shall we accept good from God, and not trouble?"

For days and nights that stretched into weeks, Job's friends came to sit with him in silence, contemplating the enormity of his suffering. They could not fathom why such calamity had befallen their righteous friend. But Job, in his agony and confusion, wrestled with his faith and with the Almighty.

"Why do the wicked live on, growing old and increasing in power?" Job cried out to the heavens. "Yet the innocent suffer and are crushed under the weight of despair!"

And in the silence that followed, a voice spoke to Job from the whirlwind, "Who is this that obscures my plans with words without knowledge? Brace yourself like a man; I will question you, and you shall answer me."

Thus began a dialogue between Job and the Almighty—a conversation that would test not only Job's endurance but also his understanding of divine justice and mercy.

Through the trials that ensued, Job's faith remained unshaken, though his heart and body were broken. His friends offered explanations and accusations, but Job sought solace in the knowledge that his Redeemer lives, and that one day he would see God.

And so, in the land of Uz, amidst the wreckage of his former life and the relentless pain that gripped his body, Job endured—a testament to the enduring strength of the human spirit and the unwavering faith in the face of suffering.

1. **Faith and Integrity:** Job is portrayed as a man of unwavering faith and integrity, even in the face of immense suffering and loss. His initial response to calamity—"The Lord gave and the Lord has taken away; may the name of the Lord be praised"—highlights his profound trust in God regardless of circumstances.
2. **Testing of Faith:** The narrative explores the concept of faith being tested through adversity. Job's steadfastness under extreme trials challenges the notion that faithfulness to God is solely based on receiving blessings.
3. **Divine Justice and Suffering:** Job's suffering raises questions about the nature of divine justice. His friends' attempts to explain his suffering as punishment for sin are countered by Job's innocence, leading to a deeper exploration of the complexities of suffering and God's sovereignty.
4. **Human Limitations in Understanding:** The dialogue between Job and God emphasizes human limitations in comprehending the ways of the divine. Job's questions and God's response illustrate that there are aspects of God's plans and wisdom that exceed

human understanding.

5. **Redemption and Restoration:** Despite Job's profound suffering, he maintains hope in redemption. He expresses confidence in his Redeemer and believes in eventual restoration, demonstrating resilience in the face of despair.

6. **Friendship and Support:** Job's friends initially provide silent support, but their attempts to explain his suffering often miss the mark. This underscores the importance of genuine empathy and understanding in times of crisis.

7. **Endurance and Perseverance:** Job's endurance through his trials serves as a testament to the resilience of the human spirit. His willingness to engage with his suffering and seek understanding from God exemplifies perseverance in faith.

5(b).

Paul's Perseverance in His Ministry

(2 Corinthians 11:23-28)

In the bustling city of Corinth, amidst the cobbled streets and vibrant marketplaces, Paul sat in a humble room, the evening sun casting long shadows through the narrow window. The air was thick with the scent of spices and the distant sound of merchants haggling echoed faintly in the background.

Paul, a man of weathered features and intense eyes, sat reflecting on the journey that had brought him to this moment. His thoughts drifted to the countless trials he had endured in service to Christ, trials that shaped not only his faith but also the very fabric of his being.

With a sigh, Paul began to recount his experiences, not out of arrogance but out of a deep conviction that his weaknesses and sufferings were a testament to the strength of his faith.

"Whatever anyone else dares to boast about—I am speaking as a fool—I also dare to boast about," Paul murmured to himself, his voice tinged with a mix of weariness and resolve.

"Are they Hebrews? So am I. Are they Israelites? So am I. Are they Abraham's descendants? So am I," Paul continued, his words gaining momentum as memories flooded his mind.

"Are they servants of Christ? (I am out of my mind to talk like this.) I am more," Paul declared with a wry smile, acknowledging the absurdity of comparing hardships for the sake of boasting.

"I have worked much harder, been in prison more frequently, been flogged more severely, and been exposed to death again and again," Paul recounted, his voice growing solemn as he recalled each ordeal with vivid clarity.

"Five times I received from the Jews the forty lashes minus one. Three times I was beaten with rods, once I was pelted with stones," Paul listed off, his hand unconsciously tracing the scars that crisscrossed his body.

"Three times I was shipwrecked, I spent a night and a day in the open sea," Paul continued, his voice steady despite the turmoil of memories.

"I have been constantly on the move. I have been in danger from rivers, in danger from bandits, in danger from my fellow Jews, in danger from Gentiles; in danger in the city, in danger in the country, in danger at sea; and in danger from false believers," Paul recounted, each danger etched into his soul like a map of his missionary journeys.

"I have labored and toiled and have often gone without sleep; I have known hunger and thirst and have often gone without food; I have been cold and naked," Paul confessed, his gaze distant as he remembered the nights spent in prayer and the days spent preaching amidst adversity.

"Besides everything else, I face daily the pressure of my concern for all the churches," Paul admitted, his heart heavy with the weight of responsibility for the fledgling communities of believers scattered across the lands.

"Who is weak, and I do not feel weak? Who is led into sin, and I do not inwardly burn?" Paul questioned, his voice trembling slightly with emotion as he reflected on the struggles and temptations faced by those he shepherded.

"If I must boast, I will boast of the things that show my weakness," Paul concluded, his tone resolute. For in his weakness, he found strength—not his own, but the strength of the God and Father of the Lord Jesus, who sustained him through every trial and hardship.

"The God and Father of the Lord Jesus, who is to be praised forever, knows that I am not lying," Paul affirmed, his faith unwavering as he spoke.

"In Damascus, the governor under King Aretas had the city of the Damascenes guarded in order to arrest me. But I was lowered in a basket from a window in the wall and slipped through his hands," Paul recalled with a faint smile, remembering the miraculous escape that exemplified God's divine intervention in his life.

As the sun dipped below the horizon and darkness settled over

Corinth, Paul bowed his head in prayer, thanking God for the grace that sustained him through every trial and for the privilege of serving Christ, despite the hardships endured.

And in that humble room in Corinth, amidst the echoes of a bustling city, Paul's spirit remained steadfast, his faith unshaken—a testament to the enduring power of God's love and the resilience of the human spirit in the face of adversity.

1. **Strength in Weakness**: Paul's life exemplifies that true strength comes not from human accomplishments or abilities, but from acknowledging one's weaknesses and relying on God's strength. Despite enduring immense hardships—imprisonment, beatings, shipwrecks—Paul found his resilience in surrendering to God's grace.

2. **Endurance and Perseverance**: Through Paul's trials, we learn the importance of endurance and perseverance in the face of adversity. He didn't give up on his mission despite constant dangers and personal sufferings. His commitment to spreading the gospel remained unwavering, showing us that steadfast faith can endure even the toughest challenges.

3. **Humility in Service**: Despite his impressive credentials and experiences, Paul approached his ministry with humility. He didn't boast about his achievements but rather acknowledged his weaknesses and attributed any success to God's grace. This humility in service teaches us to prioritize God's glory over personal recognition.

4. **Trust in God's Providence**: Paul's escape from Damascus in a basket is a vivid example of trusting in God's providence. It reminds us that God is sovereign over all circumstances, and even in the midst of danger, His plan prevails. Paul's life encourages us to trust God's guidance and provision, even when situations seem dire.

5. **Concern for Others**: Paul's deep concern for the well-being of the churches he founded demonstrates his selfless love and dedication to nurturing the faith of others. His example challenges us to care for the spiritual growth and welfare of fellow believers, even amidst our own trials and challenges.

6. **Faith in God's Faithfulness**: Throughout his journeys, Paul's faith in God's faithfulness remained unshaken. He believed in God's promises and relied on His strength to carry him through every trial. This unwavering faith serves as an inspiration for us to trust in God's faithfulness, knowing that He is always with us, no matter the circumstances.

Chapter 6

Adaptability and Innovation

Adaptability and innovation are twin pillars crucial for navigating the dynamic landscapes of business, technology, and society at large. In today's rapidly evolving world, organizations and individuals alike must possess these qualities to not only survive but thrive.

Adaptability encompasses the ability to adjust to new conditions swiftly and effectively. It involves being flexible in one's thinking and approach, ready to pivot when necessary. Organizations that embrace adaptability can respond adeptly to changes in the market, technological advancements, or unforeseen challenges. Whether it's a shift in consumer preferences, regulatory changes, or economic downturns, adaptable businesses are better equipped to weather storms and seize emerging opportunities. Moreover, adaptable leaders foster resilient teams capable of innovation and creativity in problem-solving.

Innovation complements adaptability by driving progress and differentiation. It involves the creation of new ideas, products, or processes that add value and propel growth. Innovation thrives in environments that encourage experimentation, collaboration, and a willingness to challenge the status quo. Businesses that prioritize innovation can disrupt industries, capture new markets, and stay ahead of competitors. From breakthrough technologies to novel business models, innovation fuels transformation and secures long-term relevance.

The synergy between adaptability and innovation is particularly evident in tech-driven sectors. Companies like Apple and Tesla exemplify how constant adaptation to technological advancements coupled with relentless innovation leads to market leadership and sustained growth. Moreover, in fields like healthcare and education, adaptability and innovation are driving forces behind improving service delivery, enhancing patient care, and revolutionizing learning experiences.

On an individual level, adaptability and innovation are increasingly valued traits in the workplace. Professionals who embrace lifelong learning, welcome change, and think creatively are more likely to succeed in today's fluid job market.

6(a).

Joseph's Management During Famine

(Genesis 41)

In the heart of Egypt, amid the bustling streets and grand palaces, Pharaoh's dreams echoed through the land like whispers of fate. Joseph, once a captive in the depths of a dungeon, now stood before the ruler of the greatest empire of his time.

The dreams had troubled Pharaoh deeply. Two visions, each vivid and foreboding, had haunted his sleep. As he recounted them to Joseph, the young Hebrew listened intently, his gaze unwavering as the ruler of Egypt detailed the images of fat cows devoured by lean ones, and healthy grains consumed by scorched ones.

Upon hearing Pharaoh's dreams, Joseph's voice resonated with certainty, "The dreams of Pharaoh are one and the same. God has revealed to Pharaoh what he is about to do." With divine clarity, Joseph interpreted the dreams: seven years of abundant harvest would be followed by seven years of devastating famine. It was a prophecy of prosperity and hardship intertwined, a testament to the inevitable cycle of life.

Impressed by Joseph's wisdom and discernment, Pharaoh saw in him a rare gift—an interpreter of dreams blessed by the spirit of God. He wasted no time in elevating Joseph from prisoner to steward of Egypt, clothed in robes of fine linen and adorned with a gold chain, second only to Pharaoh himself.

"Make way!" the people cried as Joseph rode through the streets in a chariot, a symbol of his newfound authority. He oversaw the collection and storage of grain during the years of abundance, amassing quantities that stretched beyond measure, like the sands of the sea.

As the years unfolded according to Joseph's prophecy, Egypt flourished amidst plenty while neighboring lands succumbed to famine. Joseph's foresight saved Egypt from ruin, as people from all corners of the known world journeyed to Egypt, seeking grain that Joseph had stored in abundance.

In those years, Joseph was not only a steward of grain but also a builder of a new life. He married Asenath, daughter of Potiphera, and they bore two sons, Manasseh and Ephraim. Each name carried meaning—Manasseh, a reminder of forgetting past troubles, and Ephraim, a symbol of fruitfulness in a land once marked by suffering.

Thus, Joseph's journey from the depths of captivity to the heights of power unfolded against the backdrop of Pharaoh's dreams. His story became a testament to the intertwining forces of fate, faith, and foresight—where adaptability and innovation, guided by divine wisdom, led one man to change the course of a nation and shape its destiny for generations to come.

1. **Foresight and Preparedness:** Joseph's interpretation of Pharaoh's dreams and his subsequent plan to store grain during years of plenty exemplify the value of foresight. By anticipating future events and planning accordingly, Joseph not only saved Egypt from famine but also positioned it as a bastion of prosperity in a time of widespread hardship. This underscores the importance of strategic thinking and preparedness in both personal and organizational contexts.

2. **Faith and Divine Guidance:** Throughout Joseph's journey, his faith in God's guidance and providence remained steadfast. He attributed his ability to interpret dreams not to his own wisdom alone but to God's revelation. This faith sustained him through adversity and empowered him to rise above circumstances that seemed insurmountable. Joseph's story reminds us of the strength that faith can provide in navigating uncertain times and making impactful decisions.

3. **Resilience and Adaptability:** From being sold into slavery by his own brothers to enduring false accusations and imprisonment, Joseph exhibited remarkable resilience. His ability to adapt to changing circumstances, maintain integrity, and seize opportunities ultimately led to his elevation to a position of immense influence. Joseph's resilience teaches us the importance of perseverance in the face of adversity and the capacity to turn challenges into opportunities for growth and advancement.

4. **Legacy of Integrity and Leadership:** Joseph's leadership was characterized by integrity, wisdom, and a commitment to the well-being of others. His management of Egypt's resources during the famine not only secured the nation's survival but also set a standard of compassionate governance. Joseph's legacy serves as a model of leadership that prioritizes service, foresight, and ethical decision-making for the benefit of society.

6(b).

Paul's Adaptive Approach in Ministry

(Acts 17:22-34)

The bustling city of Athens buzzed with life as Paul, a traveler and teacher of the gospel, found himself standing amidst the learned men of the Areopagus. This council, known for its intellectual debates and discussions on matters of philosophy and religion, now turned its attention to the foreigner who dared to challenge their beliefs.

Paul, undeterred by the grandeur of the setting or the gravity of the audience, began his address with a keen observation. "People of Athens! I see that in every way you are very religious," he proclaimed, his voice carrying with it a blend of respect and conviction.

"As I walked around your city," Paul continued, "I noticed an altar with the inscription: to an unknown god. You worship without knowing the true nature of the one you seek. This, I am here to proclaim to you."

With a calm demeanor, Paul articulated his message of faith in a God who transcended human understanding. "The God who made the world and everything in it," he declared, "is the Lord of heaven and earth. He does not dwell in temples built by human hands, nor does he require offerings from us. Rather, he is the giver of life and breath to all."

The council members listened intently as Paul expounded on the divine sovereignty over nations and the providential ordering of human history. "God has orchestrated our existence," Paul asserted, "so that we might seek him, though he is not far from any of us. In him, we live and move and have our being."

Quoting their own poets, Paul emphasized the folly of worshipping idols crafted from earthly materials. "Since we are God's offspring," he reasoned, "we ought not to liken him to gold or silver or stone, shaped by human artistry."

Paul's words resonated deeply with some in the assembly, sparking curiosity and conviction. "God once overlooked such ignorance," Paul continued, "but now calls all people to repentance. He has appointed a day when justice will prevail through a man whom he has raised from the dead."

Upon hearing of resurrection, a concept foreign yet intriguing, the council's response was divided. Some scoffed at the notion, while others expressed a desire to hear more. Paul, sensing the conclusion of his discourse, left the Areopagus, leaving behind a gathering in contemplation.

Among those who embraced Paul's teaching were Dionysius, a member of the council, and Damaris, a woman of influence. Alongside them, many others chose to follow Paul and believe in the message of hope and redemption he brought from afar.

Thus, in the heart of Athens, amidst the marble columns and scholarly debates, Paul's proclamation echoed—a testament to the power of faith, the call to repentance, and the transformative message of resurrection that would forever change the lives of those who heard it.

1. **Respectful Engagement:** Paul begins his address by acknowledging the Athenians' religiosity and cultural practices. Despite their worship of many gods, including an altar to an "unknown god," Paul respects their beliefs and uses this as a starting point to introduce the gospel. This approach teaches us the importance of understanding and respecting different cultural contexts when sharing our faith or beliefs.

2. **Revealing the True Nature of God:** Paul emphasizes that the God he proclaims is not confined to temples or idols but is the creator of the universe, the giver of life, and intimately involved in human affairs. This challenges the Athenians' perception of gods as limited and anthropomorphic, inviting them to consider a higher, transcendent deity. The lesson here is about articulating the core tenets of faith in a clear and relatable manner, addressing misconceptions with grace and truth.

3. **Calling to Repentance and Transformation:** Paul boldly calls for repentance, urging the Athenians to turn from idolatry and embrace the truth of God's sovereignty and salvation through

Christ. He connects this call to repentance with the promise of judgment and resurrection, highlighting the urgency and eternal consequences of their response to the gospel. This teaches us the importance of proclaiming not just God's love and grace but also the need for repentance and personal transformation.

4. **Response and Transformation:** The varied responses from the Athenian council—some scoffed, others desired further discussion, and some embraced faith—illustrate the different ways people receive the gospel message. Paul's willingness to engage and his trust in the Holy Spirit's work demonstrate the importance of planting seeds of faith with patience and perseverance, trusting that God will bring about transformation in hearts and minds.

5. **Impact and Endurance of Faith:** The conversion of Dionysius, Damaris, and others underscores the transformative power of Paul's proclamation. Their decision to follow Christ amidst the intellectual and cultural challenges of Athens highlights the enduring impact of faithful witness and the potential for profound spiritual change in any cultural setting.

Part III

Building and Sustaining Effective Teams

Chapter 7

Servant Leadership

Servant leadership is a philosophy that emphasizes collaboration, empathy, and ethical use of power to achieve meaningful results. Coined by Robert K. Greenleaf in the 1970s, it contrasts traditional leadership paradigms by prioritizing the needs of others over the leader's own interests. At its core, servant leadership is about serving first and leading second, where the leader's primary goal is to support and enrich the lives of their followers, enabling them to reach their fullest potential.

Key characteristics of servant leadership include empathy, listening, stewardship, and commitment to the growth of people. Empathy is crucial as it allows leaders to understand and connect with their team members on a personal level, fostering trust and a positive working environment. Listening goes beyond hearing words; it involves active engagement to comprehend the concerns, ideas, and aspirations of others.

Stewardship reflects the leader's responsibility to manage resources and talents entrusted to them for the greater good of the organization and its members. Servant leaders prioritize the development and well-being of their team members, recognizing that by empowering others and enabling their success, the organization as a whole thrives.

Servant leadership also emphasizes the ethical use of power. Rather than wielding authority for personal gain or control, servant leaders use their influence to uplift others and promote fairness and justice within their teams and organizations. This approach fosters a culture of collaboration and mutual respect, where every team member feels valued and motivated to contribute their best.

Furthermore, servant leadership encourages a long-term perspective on decision-making and organizational success. By investing in the growth and development of individuals, servant leaders cultivate a sustainable and resilient organizational culture that can adapt to challenges and thrive in changing environments.

Jesus Washing the Disciples' Feet

(John 13:1-17)

It was a warm evening, the air thick with the scent of freshly baked bread and the anticipation of the approaching Passover Festival. Jesus, knowing his time on earth was drawing to a close, gathered with his disciples for a final meal. The atmosphere was heavy with both the joy of fellowship and the shadow of betrayal.

Seated around the low table, the disciples shared in the meal, their thoughts drifting to the events that were unfolding. Judas, under the sway of darkness, had already set in motion the events that would lead to Jesus' arrest and crucifixion.

In the midst of this solemn gathering, Jesus rose from his place. His movements were deliberate, calm, and filled with a quiet resolve. Removing his outer garment, he took up a towel and tied it around his waist, the attire of a servant. The disciples watched in silence, puzzled by their Lord's actions.

With a basin of water in hand, Jesus knelt before each disciple, his hands tenderly washing their dusty feet. Peter, ever impulsive and outspoken, protested at first, unable to comprehend why his Lord would perform such a menial task. "Lord, are you going to wash my feet?" he questioned, his voice tinged with disbelief.

Jesus, his eyes filled with love and understanding, replied gently, "You do not realize now what I am doing, but later you will understand." Peter, overcome with reverence and humility, implored Jesus not only to wash his feet but his hands and head as well, seeking to be fully cleansed by his beloved Teacher.

Jesus, with his characteristic wisdom, explained, "Those who have had a bath need only to wash their feet; their whole body is clean." He spoke not only of physical cleanliness but also of spiritual purification, knowing that one among them would soon betray him.

When Jesus had washed all their feet, he resumed his place at the table, his demeanor unchanged despite the weight of impending events. Looking deeply into the eyes of his disciples, he posed a question that would resonate through the ages, "Do you understand what I have done for you?"

He continued, "I have set you an example that you should do as I have done for you. No servant is greater than his master." Jesus, the Teacher and Lord, had demonstrated the essence of servant leadership, showing that true greatness lies in humble service to others.

As the disciples pondered his words, they realized the profound lesson their Lord had imparted to them that evening—to love and serve one another selflessly, to emulate the humility and compassion of their Teacher. They were to carry forth this message, not just in words but in deeds, knowing they would be blessed in their obedience.

And so, in the quiet of that evening, amidst the flickering light of the oil lamps, Jesus had taught them perhaps the most powerful lesson of all—that true leadership is found in the humblest acts of service.

1. **Leadership through Service**: Jesus exemplified that true leadership is not about authority or power but about serving others selflessly. By washing his disciples' feet—a task typically reserved for servants—he demonstrated that leaders should prioritize the needs and well-being of those they lead.

2. **Humility and Compassion**: Jesus showed immense humility by performing a menial task and expressing compassion for his disciples. He set aside his status as Teacher and Lord to connect with them on a personal and humble level, fostering a deeper sense of trust and unity.

3. **Teaching by Example**: Instead of merely instructing his disciples verbally, Jesus chose to teach through action. He emphasized the importance of living out one's beliefs and values, urging his followers to emulate his humility and servant-heartedness in their own lives.

4. **Spiritual and Moral Cleansing**: Jesus' act of washing feet symbolized not only physical cleanliness but also spiritual purification. He reminded his disciples of the ongoing need for spiritual renewal and humility, acknowledging their imperfections yet offering grace and forgiveness.

5. **Unity and Brotherhood**: Through his actions, Jesus promoted a sense of equality and mutual respect among his disciples. By serving each of them equally, regardless of their status or personality, he emphasized the importance of unity and solidarity within the community of believers.

6. **Future Insight and Understanding**: Jesus recognized that his disciples might not fully grasp the significance of his actions at that moment. He assured them that they would understand later, implying that true wisdom often comes with reflection and experience.

7. **Blessings of Obedience**: Jesus concluded by promising blessings to those who follow his example of humble service. He emphasized that those who practice servant leadership will be blessed, highlighting the spiritual rewards of living a life dedicated to serving others.

7(b).

The Leadership Of Moses

(Exodus 18)

Jethro, the wise priest of Midian, had journeyed through the wilderness to visit Moses, his son-in-law, near the mountain of God. The desert air shimmered with heat as Jethro and his entourage approached the camp where Moses resided with the Israelites.

Moses had sent his wife Zipporah and their sons ahead to Jethro, who welcomed them warmly into his care. Now, as Jethro arrived, Moses came out to meet him, his face radiant with both fatigue and joy at seeing his trusted father-in-law.

"Moses!" Jethro exclaimed, embracing him. "It is good to see you, my son."

"Moses bowed down and kissed him, and they greeted each other warmly before entering the tent where they could speak in privacy.

Inside the tent, seated on woven mats, Moses recounted the incredible journey since they last met. He spoke of the plagues that had befallen Egypt, the parting of the Red Sea, and the miraculous provisions in the desert.

Jethro listened intently, his eyes reflecting both pride and concern for Moses and his people. When Moses finished speaking, Jethro sighed deeply and said, "Praise be to the Lord, who has shown such great mercy to His people."

Moses nodded solemnly, grateful for Jethro's understanding and support.

The next day, Moses resumed his role as judge among the people. From dawn till dusk, they stood before him, seeking his counsel and judgment in matters large and small. Jethro observed quietly from a distance, his brow furrowed in thought.

When evening descended, Jethro approached Moses, concern etched on his face. "Moses, my son," he began gently, "what is this that you are doing for the people? Why do you sit alone as judge, while all these people wait upon you?"

Moses sighed wearily. "They come to me seeking God's will. When disputes arise, I must decide between them according to His laws."

Jethro nodded knowingly but shook his head. "This is not good, Moses. You will wear yourself out, and the people too. The burden is too heavy for you to bear alone."

Moses looked at Jethro, surprised yet open to his counsel.

"Listen to me," Jethro continued, his voice firm yet kind. "You must be the people's representative before God, but appoint capable men to assist you. Choose men of integrity, who fear God and abhor dishonest gain. Let them judge the simpler matters, only bringing the most difficult cases to you. This way, they will share the burden with you, and you will be able to endure."

Moses considered Jethro's words carefully. They resonated deeply within him, a wise solution to the overwhelming task before him.

"May God be with you in this decision," Jethro added, his eyes gentle yet unwavering.

And so, Moses heeded Jethro's advice. He selected capable men from among the people and appointed them as leaders and judges over thousands, hundreds, fifties, and tens. They were men who feared God and were known for their honesty and wisdom.

From that day onward, the people brought their disputes to these appointed judges, who applied God's decrees and settled matters justly. Only the most difficult cases reached Moses, who guided the people according to God's will.

Jethro remained with Moses for a time, offering guidance and wisdom whenever needed. When the time came for him to depart, Moses bid farewell to his father-in-law with gratitude and respect.

"Go well, Jethro," Moses said, clasping his hands warmly. "May the Lord bless you and keep you."

With a nod and a smile, Jethro returned to his homeland, leaving Moses and the Israelites to continue their journey under God's watchful care.

1. **Leadership and Humility**: Even a great leader like Moses can benefit from the counsel of others, showing humility and openness to advice.

2. **Recognizing Limits**: Jethro highlights the importance of recognizing one's limits. Moses couldn't handle all responsibilities alone; delegation was necessary for effective governance.

3. **Effective Delegation**: Delegating tasks to capable individuals lightens the load for leaders and empowers others to contribute meaningfully.

4. **Choosing the Right People**: Selecting individuals with integrity, fear of God, and honesty ensures that delegated responsibilities are handled justly and responsibly.

5. **Fair and Just Governance**: By establishing a hierarchical system of judges, Moses ensured that disputes were resolved fairly and in accordance with divine laws.

6. **Balancing Responsibilities**: Leaders must balance their role as representatives before God with their practical duties, ensuring they can fulfill both effectively without burning out.

7. **Respect and Gratitude**: The relationship between Moses and Jethro exemplifies respect and gratitude, essential in any partnership or mentorship.

Chapter 8

Communication and Collaboration

Communication and collaboration are foundational pillars in achieving success and fostering harmonious relationships within any organization or community. Effective communication ensures that ideas, goals, and expectations are clearly articulated and understood among team members. It involves not just speaking, but active listening and feedback, creating a cycle of understanding and alignment.

In today's interconnected world, collaboration has become essential across diverse teams and disciplines. It leverages the strengths and expertise of individuals to achieve collective goals that surpass individual capabilities. Collaboration encourages creativity, innovation, and shared problem-solving, as different perspectives and insights contribute to comprehensive solutions.

Clear communication is the cornerstone of successful collaboration. It facilitates the exchange of ideas and information, ensuring everyone is on the same page regarding project objectives, timelines, and responsibilities. Miscommunication or lack thereof can lead to misunderstandings, delays, and friction among team members.

Moreover, effective collaboration relies on trust and respect among team members. When individuals feel valued and respected for their contributions, they are more likely to collaborate openly and constructively. This environment encourages brainstorming, constructive feedback, and a willingness to compromise for the greater good.

Technology plays a vital role in modern communication and collaboration, providing tools for instant messaging, video conferencing, file sharing, and project management. These tools bridge geographical barriers and enable seamless interaction among team members regardless of their location.

8(a).

Nehemiah's Communication Strategy

(Nehemiah 2:17-18)

Nehemiah stood at the Valley Gate, gazing upon the shattered remnants of Jerusalem's once mighty walls. The moonlight cast eerie shadows over the broken stones, emphasizing the desolation that surrounded him. Three days earlier, he had arrived in the city, his heart heavy with sorrow and determination.

During the quiet of the night, with only a few trusted companions by his side, Nehemiah embarked on his clandestine mission. He rode out towards the Jackal Well and the Dung Gate, tracing the perimeter of the city. Each step revealed more devastation — walls collapsed, gates reduced to ash by fire. The enormity of the task ahead weighed heavily upon him as he observed the scale of destruction.

As he moved towards the Fountain Gate and the King's Pool, Nehemiah encountered impassable rubble that blocked his path. Undeterred, he navigated through the valley, examining every fissure and gap in the walls. The silence of the night was broken only by the faint echoes of his footsteps and the occasional sound of crumbling masonry underfoot.

Returning through the Valley Gate, Nehemiah's mind raced with plans and prayers. He knew that rebuilding Jerusalem's walls was not just a physical endeavor but a spiritual calling, guided by the hand of God. Yet, he had not yet shared his intentions with anyone, waiting for the right moment.

Days later, standing before the people – Jews, priests, nobles, and officials – Nehemiah spoke with conviction born of faith and determination. "Look at the state of our city," he proclaimed, his voice carrying across the gathered crowd. "Jerusalem lies in ruins, a disgrace to our God. Let us rebuild these walls and restore our honor!"

Moved by his words and inspired by the grace of God upon Nehemiah, the people responded with unanimous resolve: "Let us start rebuilding."

But not everyone shared their zeal. Sanballat the Horonite, Tobiah the Ammonite, and Geshem the Arab, adversaries of Jerusalem, scoffed and jeered at their efforts. "Are you defying the king?" they taunted, seeking to sow doubt and division.

Nehemiah's response was unwavering, his faith resolute. "The God of heaven will grant us success," he declared boldly. "We, his servants, will rebuild. But you have no part in this holy city."

With those words, Nehemiah set the stage for a great undertaking – the rebuilding of Jerusalem's walls – a testament to faith, courage, and the unwavering determination to restore what was lost.

1. **Vision and Purpose**: Nehemiah's mission to inspect Jerusalem's walls underscores the importance of having a clear vision and purpose. He saw beyond the desolation to envision a rebuilt city that would honor God and restore dignity to its people.

2. **Courage in Adversity**: Despite facing overwhelming destruction and opposition, Nehemiah displayed courage and resolve. He undertook a dangerous nighttime inspection, demonstrating his commitment to understanding the scale of the task ahead.

3. **Faith and Guidance**: Nehemiah's actions were guided by faith in God's hand and divine guidance. His prayerful approach and reliance on God's will exemplify faith-driven leadership, acknowledging that spiritual strength is essential in facing daunting challenges.

4. **Strategic Planning**: Nehemiah's careful inspection of the walls and gates of Jerusalem reflects strategic planning and assessment. Understanding the extent of damage enabled him to formulate a comprehensive rebuilding strategy.

5. **Leadership and Communication**: Nehemiah's ability to communicate effectively rallied the people around a common goal. His impassioned speech galvanized support and united

diverse groups – Jews, priests, nobles, and officials – to commit to the rebuilding effort.

6. **Resilience in the Face of Opposition**: Nehemiah encountered resistance and mockery from adversaries like Sanballat, Tobiah, and Geshem. His steadfast response and refusal to be deterred illustrate resilience in the face of adversity.

7. **Inclusivity and Unity**: Nehemiah's leadership was inclusive, involving all segments of society in the rebuilding process. By uniting people from various backgrounds, he fostered a sense of unity and collective responsibility.

8. **Divine Providence**: Throughout Nehemiah's journey, the belief in divine providence is evident. His confidence that God would grant success bolstered morale and strengthened resolve among the rebuilding efforts.

8(b).

Paul's Letters and Collaboration with Early Churches

(Various Epistles)

Paul's letters to the early churches, found in the New Testament of the Bible, stand as foundational texts that not only address theological issues but also reveal profound insights into the dynamics of early Christian communities and Paul's role as a leader and collaborator. These epistles—Romans, Corinthians, Galatians, Ephesians, Philippians, Colossians, Thessalonians, Timothy, Titus, and Philemon—capture Paul's efforts to guide, encourage, and correct these fledgling churches spread across the Roman Empire.

Paul, formerly Saul of Tarsus, underwent a dramatic conversion on the road to Damascus, where he encountered the risen Christ (Acts 9:1-19). This encounter marked the beginning of his journey as an apostle to the Gentiles, chosen to proclaim the gospel and establish communities of believers outside the Jewish context. His letters, therefore, serve not only as theological treatises but also as practical guides for these diverse and growing congregations.

One of the key themes in Paul's letters is unity within the body of Christ. Despite the varied backgrounds and cultural differences among the early Christians, Paul emphasizes the importance of unity based on their shared faith in Jesus Christ. In his letter to the Ephesians, for example, Paul writes about the unity of the Spirit in the bond of peace (Ephesians 4:3), urging them to maintain unity amidst diversity and to live in a manner worthy of their calling.

Furthermore, Paul addresses specific issues and challenges faced by these churches. In the Corinthian correspondence, he tackles divisions within the church, immorality among believers, and misunderstandings about spiritual gifts. Through his letters, Paul provides pastoral care and practical advice, seeking to build up these communities in faith and righteousness.

Paul's letters also highlight his collaborative leadership style. Despite his authority as an apostle, Paul often refers to himself as a servant or a fellow worker alongside his colleagues such as Timothy, Titus, and Silas. He values their partnership in ministry and entrusts them with important tasks, illustrating his belief in shared responsibility and mutual encouragement in the mission of spreading the gospel.

Moreover, Paul's letters reflect his deep concern for the spiritual growth and maturity of believers. In his letter to the Philippians, he expresses his joy in their partnership in the gospel (Philippians 1:5) and encourages them to live lives worthy of Christ's gospel, filled with humility, unity, and joy despite their circumstances.

Another significant aspect of Paul's letters is his theological depth and exposition. In the letter to the Romans, for instance, Paul presents a comprehensive explanation of the gospel, emphasizing justification by faith and the inclusion of both Jews and Gentiles in God's plan of salvation. His writings in Galatians challenge legalism and affirm the freedom believers have in Christ, while in Colossians, he exalts Christ's supremacy and warns against deceptive philosophies.

1. **Unity in Christ**: Paul emphasizes the importance of unity among believers. Despite diverse backgrounds and cultural differences, he calls for unity based on their shared faith in Jesus Christ (Ephesians 4:3). This unity is not superficial but grounded in the Spirit and essential for the effectiveness of the Church's witness.

2. **Pastoral Care and Practical Advice**: Paul addresses specific issues within the early churches, such as divisions, immorality, and misunderstandings about spiritual gifts. His letters provide pastoral guidance and practical advice on how to live out the Christian faith in everyday life, promoting righteousness and harmony among believers.

3. **Collaborative Leadership**: Paul exemplifies a collaborative leadership style, despite his authority as an apostle. He often refers to himself as a servant or fellow worker alongside his colleagues like Timothy, Titus, and Silas. Paul values partnership in ministry, encouraging mutual support and shared responsibility in spreading the gospel and building up the Church.

4. **Spiritual Growth and Maturity**: Paul demonstrates deep concern

for the spiritual growth and maturity of believers. In his letters, he encourages Christians to grow in their faith, to live lives worthy of their calling in Christ, and to bear fruit in love and good works. His letters to the Philippians, for example, highlight the joy of partnership in the gospel and the pursuit of Christ-like humility and unity.

5. **Theological Depth and Exposition**: Paul's letters are rich in theological content, presenting comprehensive explanations of key doctrines such as justification by faith (Romans), freedom in Christ (Galatians), and Christ's supremacy (Colossians). He confronts false teachings and affirms essential truths of the Christian faith, providing a solid foundation for believers to understand and defend their beliefs.

6. **Application to Today's Context**: While written in a specific historical and cultural context, Paul's teachings and principles can be applied to contemporary issues and challenges faced by the Church. His emphasis on love, grace, and the transforming power of the gospel remains relevant for guiding Christian communities and individuals in navigating life's complexities with faith and integrity.

Chapter 9

Conflict Resolution and Unity

Conflict resolution and unity are essential components of a cohesive and productive society. At its core, conflict resolution involves addressing disagreements or disputes in a manner that promotes understanding, collaboration, and mutual respect among individuals or groups. This process is crucial in fostering unity because it aims to reconcile differences and build bridges rather than deepen divides.

One of the fundamental principles of effective conflict resolution is communication. Clear, open, and respectful communication allows parties to express their perspectives, concerns, and emotions constructively. Active listening is equally important, as it demonstrates empathy and a willingness to understand the other party's point of view. By creating a space for dialogue and exchange, conflicts can be de-escalated and solutions can be sought collaboratively.

Moreover, conflict resolution strategies often emphasize negotiation and compromise. Finding common ground and seeking mutually acceptable solutions can lead to resolutions that satisfy the needs and interests of all parties involved. This process requires patience, flexibility, and a focus on long-term outcomes rather than short-term victories.

In the context of larger communities or societies, conflict resolution contributes significantly to unity by fostering a sense of inclusivity and belonging. When conflicts are managed effectively, individuals and groups feel heard and respected, which enhances trust and cooperation. This, in turn, strengthens social cohesion and promotes a shared sense of purpose and identity.

Leadership plays a critical role in promoting conflict resolution and unity within organizations and communities. Leaders who prioritize mediation, dialogue, and reconciliation create environments where differences are seen as opportunities for growth rather than sources of division. By modeling constructive conflict resolution behaviors, leaders inspire others to approach disagreements with empathy and a commitment to finding common ground.

Ultimately, conflict resolution is not about eliminating differences but about managing them in a way that promotes unity and collaboration. It requires a commitment to dialogue, understanding, and compromise, guided by principles of fairness and respect. When societies prioritize these principles, they cultivate environments where diversity is celebrated, relationships are strengthened, and collective goals are pursued with shared determination.

9(a).

Jesus And the Adulterous Woman

(John 8:1-11)

The sun had just begun its ascent over the rooftops of Jerusalem as Jesus made his way to the Temple Mount. The city stirred awake with the bustling sounds of early morning merchants setting up their stalls and families making their way to the temple courts for prayer and teaching.

As Jesus entered the temple area, a hush fell over the crowd. Word had spread quickly of his arrival, and soon people from all corners gathered around him, eager to hear his words. He sat down, a gesture of authority and readiness to teach.

But amidst the eager crowd, there was a stir of commotion. The teachers of the law and the Pharisees pushed through, dragging a woman with them. She stumbled forward, disheveled and frightened, her eyes darting around the crowd. The Pharisees positioned her in the center, before Jesus, and spoke with calculated venom in their voices.

"Teacher," one of them called out, "this woman was caught in the act of adultery. In the Law, Moses commanded us to stone such women. Now what do you say?"

Their voices dripped with accusation, their eyes keenly watching Jesus for his response. This was not a question asked out of genuine curiosity but a trap set with cunning precision. They sought to test him, to trap him into saying something they could use against him.

Jesus did not immediately respond. Instead, he stooped down and began to write on the ground with his finger, as if he had not heard them. The Pharisees exchanged puzzled glances, impatient for his answer. They pressed him further, repeating their question.

Finally, Jesus stood up, his gaze steady and unwavering. "Let any one of you who is without sin be the first to throw a stone at her."

With these words, a silence fell over the crowd. Jesus's response cut through the tension like a sharp blade. The Pharisees, taken aback by his wisdom and authority, looked at each other uncomfortably. One by one, starting with the eldest, they began to walk away, their stones left untouched on the ground.

The woman, trembling, remained standing where she had been brought. Her eyes were fixed on Jesus, unsure of what would come next. He knelt down again and continued writing on the ground, the crowd holding its breath.

When Jesus finally looked up, only the woman remained. "Woman, where are they? Has no one condemned you?"

"No one, sir," she whispered, tears streaming down her face.

"Then neither do I condemn you," Jesus declared. "Go now and leave your life of sin."

With these words of grace and forgiveness, the woman felt a weight lifted from her shoulders. She left the temple that day not just forgiven but transformed by the encounter with Jesus, who had shown her mercy when others sought judgment.

The crowd dispersed, murmuring among themselves about the extraordinary events they had witnessed. Jesus remained in the temple, his teaching continuing to resonate in the hearts of those who had gathered around him.

As the day progressed, news of Jesus's compassion and wisdom spread throughout Jerusalem, touching lives and stirring hearts with the promise of redemption and grace.

1. **Grace and Forgiveness**: Jesus's response to the woman, "Neither do I condemn you," exemplifies radical forgiveness and grace. It teaches us that no matter our past mistakes or sins, there is always an opportunity for redemption and a new beginning through God's mercy.

2. **Judgment and Hypocrisy**: Jesus's challenge to the Pharisees, "Let any one of you who is without sin be the first to throw a stone,"

exposes the hypocrisy of those quick to judge others. It reminds us to examine our own hearts before condemning others, emphasizing humility and self-reflection.

3. **Empathy and Compassion**: Jesus's interaction with the woman shows deep empathy and compassion. He acknowledges her humanity, treating her with dignity despite her wrongdoing. This teaches us to approach others with empathy, seeing beyond their faults and offering compassion instead of condemnation.

4. **Courage to Stand Against Injustice**: Jesus's refusal to play into the Pharisees' trap and his defense of the woman demonstrate courage in standing against injustice. This challenges us to speak up for what is right, even when faced with opposition or pressure to conform.

5. **Freedom from Sin**: Jesus's final words to the woman, "Go now and leave your life of sin," highlight the transformative power of forgiveness. It encourages us to turn away from sinful behaviors and live in accordance with God's will, embracing a life of righteousness and obedience.

6. **Impact of Witness**: The crowd's reaction to Jesus's actions underscores the profound impact of witnessing mercy and grace in action. It prompts reflection on our own role as witnesses to God's love, inspiring others through our words and actions.

9(b).

The Council of Jerusalem

(Acts 15)

The bustling city of Jerusalem buzzed with anticipation as Paul and Barnabas arrived from Antioch. They were greeted warmly by the church leaders and elders, eager to hear firsthand about the remarkable conversions among the Gentiles. The journey had been long and fraught with discussions, but they had finally arrived at the heart of their mission: to address the divisive issue of Gentile circumcision.

The council convened in a spacious chamber, filled with apostles, elders, and prominent members of the church. Tension hung in the air as the Pharisaic faction voiced their insistence that Gentile converts adhere to Mosaic law, including circumcision. Paul and Barnabas countered passionately, arguing that salvation came through faith in Christ alone, not through adherence to Jewish customs.

After hours of debate, Peter rose to speak, his voice steady yet resolute. "Brothers," he began, "you know that God has shown no partiality. He has granted the Holy Spirit to the Gentiles, just as He did to us, cleansing their hearts through faith. Why burden them with a yoke that neither we nor our ancestors could bear?"

His words resonated deeply, silencing the room. Paul and Barnabas nodded in agreement as Peter continued, recounting his own revelation from God about the inclusion of Gentiles in His plan of salvation. The assembly listened intently, swayed by the evidence of God's work among the Gentiles.

When Peter finished, James, the brother of Jesus and a respected leader in the church, stood up. "Brothers," he addressed them, "Simon has spoken rightly. The words of the prophets affirm that God's plan includes the Gentiles. Therefore, I propose that we do not make it difficult for them. Instead, we should instruct them to abstain from idolatry, sexual immorality, and consuming blood or strangled animals."

His proposal struck a chord of unity among the council members. They collectively agreed that a letter should be sent to the Gentile believers, affirming their acceptance and outlining these minimal requirements. The decision was not just about doctrine but about fostering unity and embracing the diversity within the growing Christian community.

With unity restored, the council drafted the letter, which would be delivered to Antioch, Syria, and Cilicia by Judas and Silas, trusted leaders among the believers. The letter emphasized the essentials of faith and encouraged the Gentile converts to remain steadfast in their newfound freedom in Christ.

As the letter was read aloud to the assembly, relief and joy spread through the church in Jerusalem. The decision brought clarity and reassurance to the Gentile believers and strengthened the bonds of fellowship across regions. Judas and Silas departed with the letter, accompanied by Paul and Barnabas, who were commended by the entire church to continue their mission of strengthening and encouraging the churches.

The council's decision marked a pivotal moment in the early church, setting a precedent for navigating theological differences with grace and wisdom. It underscored the importance of unity amidst diversity and the centrality of faith in Christ as the unifying force among believers.

1. **Salvation by Grace through Faith**: The council affirmed that salvation is not attained through adherence to laws or rituals, but through faith in Jesus Christ. This reaffirmed the core Christian belief that salvation is a gift from God, available to all who believe, regardless of ethnicity or cultural background.

2. **Inclusion and Acceptance**: The decision emphasized the inclusion of Gentile believers into the Christian community without imposing unnecessary burdens. It showed that God's grace extends to all people, and that cultural or religious differences should not be barriers to fellowship.

3. **Unity Amidst Diversity**: Despite differing opinions among the apostles and elders, the council reached a unified decision that

respected diversity within the church. This unity was not superficial but rooted in a shared commitment to the gospel and mutual respect for one another's perspectives.

4. **Wisdom in Decision-Making**: The council's deliberations were marked by careful consideration of scriptural teachings, past experiences of God's work, and practical implications for the church. It demonstrated the importance of seeking God's guidance and wisdom in resolving theological and doctrinal issues.

5. **Fostering Fellowship and Encouragement**: The council's decision was aimed at fostering unity and strengthening fellowship among believers. The letter sent to the Gentile believers in Antioch, Syria, and Cilicia was not just a doctrinal statement but a source of encouragement and affirmation of their faith journey.

6. **Leadership and Humility**: Leaders like Peter and James exemplified humility and leadership by listening to others, speaking with authority grounded in faith and experience, and guiding the church with wisdom and compassion.

7. **Mission and Evangelism**: The decision supported the mission of spreading the gospel to all nations by removing unnecessary barriers for Gentile believers. It highlighted the church's commitment to sharing the message of salvation with the world, reflecting God's desire for all people to come to know Him.

Part IV

Legacy and Impact

Chapter 10

Mentorship and Succession Planning

Mentorship and succession planning play crucial roles in the sustainable development and growth of organizations across various sectors. These practices are integral to ensuring continuity, fostering leadership skills, and transferring knowledge from experienced individuals to emerging talents.

Mentorship is a relationship-based developmental process where experienced professionals (mentors) guide less experienced individuals (mentees) in their personal and professional growth. This mentor-mentee dynamic serves multiple purposes: it accelerates learning, provides valuable feedback, and offers career guidance that helps mentees navigate challenges and capitalize on opportunities.

In the context of succession planning, organizations strategically identify and develop individuals who have the potential to fill key roles in the future. This proactive approach ensures that when leaders retire, resign, or move on, there are capable successors ready to step into their shoes seamlessly. Succession planning is not just about filling vacancies but about cultivating a pipeline of talent equipped with the skills, knowledge, and experience necessary to lead effectively.

The synergy between mentorship and succession planning is profound. Mentors often play pivotal roles in grooming potential successors by imparting wisdom, sharing experiences, and providing exposure to leadership roles. Through structured mentorship programs embedded within broader succession plans, organizations not only develop individual talent but also cultivate a culture of continuous learning and development.

Moreover, mentorship fosters a sense of loyalty and commitment among employees, as mentees feel valued and supported in their career aspirations. This can lead to higher employee engagement, retention, and overall organizational performance.

For mentorship and succession planning to be effective, organizations must invest in creating formalized programs, aligning mentorship goals with strategic objectives, and measuring outcomes to ensure continuous improvement. By nurturing talent through mentorship and preparing them through succession planning, organizations can mitigate risks associated with leadership transitions and position themselves for sustained success in an ever-evolving business landscape.

10(a).

Moses Mentoring Joshua

(Deuteronomy 34:9)

In the quiet solitude of the desert, the wind whispered through the tents of the Israelites, carrying with it the weight of transition. Moses, the venerable leader who had shepherded them through the wilderness for decades, knew his time was drawing near. He had led them out of Egypt, witnessed miracles, and stood before the Almighty on Mount Sinai. Now, as the days of his life waned, he looked to his trusted protege, Joshua.

"Now Joshua son of Nun," Moses said, his voice steady yet tinged with the weariness of age, "come, stand before the people and before the Lord."

Joshua, a man of strong stature and unwavering faith, approached Moses with reverence. His heart pounded with a mix of anticipation and humility as he stood before the congregation of Israelites gathered at the entrance of the Tabernacle. The sun cast long shadows across the sand, marking the solemnity of the moment.

Moses extended his weathered hands towards Joshua, the weight of leadership and divine blessing palpable in the air. "O Lord, God of the spirits of all flesh," Moses intoned, his voice echoing with authority, "appoint this man over the congregation, that he may go out before them and come in before them, and that he may lead them out and bring them in, that the congregation of the Lord may not be as sheep that have no shepherd."

As Moses spoke these words, a hush fell over the assembly. The Israelites, young and old, rich and poor, stood with heads bowed, hearts lifted in prayer. They knew the gravity of this passing of the mantle, the succession of leadership from Moses to Joshua.

In that sacred moment, something profound happened. The spirit of wisdom descended upon Joshua like a mantle of light. His eyes, once filled with uncertainty, now glowed with determination and clarity. It was a divine affirmation, a recognition that Joshua was chosen by God to lead His people forward into the promised land.

From that day forward, the Israelites listened to Joshua as they had listened to Moses. They followed him through battles and victories, through trials and triumphs. For Joshua walked in the ways of the Lord, guided by the wisdom imparted to him by Moses, and upheld by the faith of his people.

Thus, the mantle of leadership passed from Moses to Joshua, ensuring that the journey of the Israelites continued under the watchful eye and guiding hand of God.

1. **Divine Appointment and Timing**: The story underscores the importance of divine timing and appointment in leadership transitions. Moses recognized when his time to lead was coming to an end and actively prepared Joshua to take over. This highlights the significance of recognizing and accepting transitions in life and leadership with grace and wisdom.

2. **Mentorship and Succession Planning**: Moses' mentorship of Joshua exemplifies the crucial role of mentorship in preparing the next generation of leaders. Through years of guidance and experience-sharing, Moses equipped Joshua not only with skills but also with spiritual and moral grounding necessary for leadership.

3. **Humility and Reverence**: Joshua's humility and reverence towards Moses demonstrate qualities essential in a leader. Despite his upcoming leadership role, Joshua approached Moses with respect and humility, recognizing the weight of responsibility that came with leading the Israelites.

4. **Spiritual Authority and Divine Guidance**: The passing of the mantle from Moses to Joshua was accompanied by a tangible sense of divine presence and affirmation. This reinforces the belief that effective leadership is grounded in spiritual authority and guided by divine wisdom.

5. **Continuity and Unity**: The smooth transition from Moses to Joshua ensured continuity in leadership, preventing the

congregation from becoming "sheep without a shepherd." It emphasizes the importance of maintaining unity and stability within a community or organization during times of leadership change.

6. **Courage and Determination**: Joshua's transformation from a hesitant follower to a confident leader reflects the transformative power of faith, courage, and determination. His acceptance of the mantle of leadership symbolizes readiness to embrace challenges and lead his people with strength and conviction.

7. **Legacy and Vision**: The story illustrates the passing of a legacy from one leader to the next. Moses' vision for the Israelites to enter the promised land was carried forward by Joshua, highlighting the importance of leaders imparting their vision and values to ensure the continuation of their mission.

10(b).

Paul Mentoring Timothy

(1 Timothy 1:2)

In the bustling city of Ephesus, amidst the narrow streets and lively marketplaces, Paul sat in a quiet corner of his modest dwelling, parchment and quill in hand. His weathered face, etched with lines of experience and faith, softened with a fatherly smile as he began to write.

"Paul, an apostle of Christ Jesus by the command of God our Savior and of Christ Jesus our hope," he penned with deliberate strokes, his heart overflowing with a sense of divine purpose.

"To Timothy my true son in the faith," he continued, his words carrying the weight of both authority and affection. Timothy, a young disciple whom Paul had nurtured and mentored, was now entrusted with the care and guidance of the church in Ephesus— a responsibility Paul held dear.

Grace, mercy, and peace from God the Father and Christ Jesus our Lord," Paul prayed, his heart lifting these blessings over his beloved Timothy. He knew the challenges that lay ahead for the young leader—the trials of teaching, the burdens of pastoral care, and the necessity of standing firm in the face of opposition.

As Paul wrote, memories flooded his mind: the first meeting with Timothy in Lystra, the journeying together through cities and towns, the countless hours spent in prayer and study. He recalled Timothy's earnest questions, his hunger for knowledge, and his unwavering commitment to the gospel they both cherished.

"My dear Timothy," Paul continued, his voice echoing through the parchment, "do not let anyone look down on you because you are young, but set an example for the believers in speech, in conduct, in love, in faith, and in purity."

Paul knew the importance of encouragement, of lifting up and empowering the next generation of leaders. He urged Timothy to embrace his calling with confidence, to lead by example, and to hold fast to the teachings passed down to him.

"You, Timothy, have been entrusted with a noble task," Paul wrote, his words a rallying cry for courage and perseverance. "Guard what has been entrusted to your care. Turn away from godless chatter and the opposing ideas of what is falsely called knowledge, which some have professed and in so doing have departed from the faith."

As he finished the letter, Paul prayed once more for Timothy's strength and wisdom. He sealed the scroll, knowing that his words carried not only instruction but also a deep-seated love for his spiritual son and a fervent hope for the flourishing of the church they both served.

Thus, in the quiet solitude of his room in Ephesus, Paul's letter to Timothy became not just a mentor's guidance but a testament to the enduring bond of faith and the transformative power of mentorship in the early Christian community.

From Paul's letter to Timothy, several key lessons on mentorship and leadership emerge:

1. **Divine Calling and Purpose**: Paul begins by emphasizing that leadership is not merely a human endeavor but a divine calling. Leaders are appointed by God and should align themselves with God's command and purpose.

2. **Relationship and Affection**: Paul's relationship with Timothy is characterized by deep affection and familial bonds. Effective mentorship is rooted in genuine care and personal investment in the growth and well-being of the mentee.

3. **Empowerment and Encouragement**: Paul encourages Timothy not to be hindered by his youth but to embrace his role with confidence. Effective mentors empower their mentees by instilling belief in their abilities and encouraging them to set an example in every aspect of their lives.

4. **Guarding the Faith**: Paul stresses the importance of guarding the teachings entrusted to Timothy. Mentorship involves passing on

not only knowledge but also values and principles that sustain faith and integrity in the face of challenges and opposition.

5. **Prayer and Spiritual Support**: Throughout the letter, Paul interweaves prayers for Timothy's strength, wisdom, and perseverance. Effective mentors provide spiritual support through prayer and personal example, recognizing that leadership in faith requires spiritual resilience.

6. **Legacy and Continuity**: Paul's mentorship of Timothy exemplifies the passing on of a spiritual legacy from one generation to the next. Effective mentorship extends beyond the immediate guidance to nurturing future leaders who will continue the work with faithfulness and dedication.

7. **Example and Integrity**: Paul urges Timothy to set an example in speech, conduct, love, faith, and purity. Effective mentors lead by example, demonstrating integrity and consistency in their words and actions, thereby inspiring and guiding their mentees.

Chapter 11

Leaving a Lasting Legacy

Leaving a lasting legacy in leadership involves more than achieving short-term success; it requires a deliberate and sustained commitment to principles that transcend individual achievements. A leader who aspires to leave a meaningful legacy focuses on cultivating enduring values, inspiring others through example, and making a positive impact that extends beyond their tenure.

Firstly, effective leadership revolves around integrity and ethical conduct. Leaders who uphold honesty, transparency, and fairness set a standard that others aspire to emulate. By consistently demonstrating integrity in decision-making and interactions, they build trust and credibility, essential elements for a lasting legacy.

Secondly, nurturing and empowering others is crucial. A legacy isn't solely about personal accomplishments but about developing future leaders. Effective mentors invest time and resources in grooming talent, imparting knowledge, and providing opportunities for growth. By empowering others to succeed and surpass their own achievements, leaders ensure their influence endures beyond their time in office.

Furthermore, vision and innovation play key roles in shaping a lasting legacy. Leaders who envision a better future, articulate a compelling vision, and innovate to solve complex challenges leave an indelible mark. They inspire followers with a sense of purpose and direction, fostering a culture of continuous improvement and adaptability.

Lastly, leaving a legacy involves community and societal impact. Leaders who prioritize serving others, promoting social justice, and contributing to the greater good leave behind a legacy of compassion and positive change. By addressing systemic issues, advocating for marginalized groups, and promoting sustainable practices, they leave a tangible imprint on society.

In essence, leaving a lasting legacy in leadership requires a blend of personal integrity, commitment to empowering others, visionary leadership, and societal impact. It's about leaving behind a world that is better because of one's leadership—where values endure, people thrive, and progress continues long after one's time in leadership has passed.

11(a).

The legacy of King David

As the sun dipped low over the hills of Jerusalem, casting long shadows across the courtyard of the palace, King David reclined on a cushioned divan, his aging frame adorned with robes befitting his royal stature. Beside him stood his son Solomon, tall and earnest, his youthful face a mirror of both anticipation and solemnity.

"Solomon, my son," David began, his voice a mixture of strength and tenderness that bespoke a lifetime of battles fought and victories won. "The time has come for me to depart from this world. But before I go, I must impart to you a charge—a charge that will guide you in the days ahead."

Solomon listened intently, his heart swelling with reverence for the father who had led Israel through triumph and turmoil,

123

establishing a kingdom renowned for its glory and righteousness.

"I am about to go the way of all the earth," David continued, his gaze fixed upon Solomon with unwavering intensity. "Therefore, be strong and courageous, for you will be the king of Israel. Act like a man—not merely in stature, but in the depth of your character."

Solomon nodded solemnly, understanding the weight of his father's words. He knew that to rule a nation as God's chosen leader required not only physical courage but moral fortitude.

"Observe what the Lord your God requires of you," David instructed, his voice resonating with the authority of one who had walked closely with the Almighty. "Walk in obedience to Him, keep His decrees and commands, His laws and regulations, as written in the Law of Moses."

The flickering torches illuminated the lines etched upon David's weathered face, lines that spoke of battles fought against enemies both external and internal, and of a faith that had endured through every trial.

"Do this," David continued, his voice softer now, yet filled with conviction, "so that you may prosper in all you do and wherever you go. And remember the promise God made to me—that as long as our descendants walk faithfully before Him with all their heart and soul, there will always be a successor on the throne of Israel."

Solomon felt the weight of his father's charge settling upon his shoulders like a royal mantle. He knew that he stood at the threshold of a great responsibility—to honor God, to lead His people with wisdom and justice, and to preserve the legacy of his father, David, the beloved king of Israel.

With a final embrace, David imparted his blessing upon Solomon, a benediction that carried the hopes and prayers of generations past and future. As the evening shadows deepened and the stars emerged in the velvet sky, father and son stood together, bound by a sacred covenant of leadership, faith, and enduring love.

And so, in the fading light of that Jerusalem evening, the legacy of David was passed to Solomon, a beacon of light and righteousness for the kingdom of Israel, destined to shine brightly through the annals of history.

1. **Courage and Character**: David emphasizes to Solomon the importance of strength and courage, not just in physical terms, but in the depth of one's character. True leadership requires moral fortitude and steadfastness in the face of challenges.

2. **Obedience to God**: Central to David's charge is the call to obedience to God's commands. He stresses the significance of living according to God's will as outlined in the Law of Moses. This underscores the importance of spiritual grounding and adherence to ethical principles in leadership.

3. **Promise and Legacy**: David reminds Solomon of God's promise— that as long as their descendants remain faithful, there will always be a successor on the throne of Israel. This highlights the enduring nature of promises made by leaders and the responsibility to ensure continuity and stability for future

generations.

4. **Responsibility and Leadership**: Solomon is entrusted with the weighty responsibility to honor God, lead with wisdom and justice, and preserve David's legacy. This illustrates the transfer of leadership and the passing down of values and vision from one generation to the next.

5. **Blessing and Covenant**: The final embrace between David and Solomon symbolizes a sacred covenant of leadership, faith, and love. Leaders should recognize the importance of imparting blessings, encouragement, and guidance to those they mentor and lead, fostering a sense of unity and shared purpose.

6. **Enduring Influence**: David's legacy serves as a beacon of light and righteousness for Israel. It exemplifies how a leader's actions and teachings can resonate across generations, shaping history and inspiring future leaders to uphold similar values of faith, courage, and obedience.

11(b).

The impact of Jesus' ministry

(Gospels)

Jesus Christ's ministry, as depicted in the Gospels of the New Testament, stands as a transformative force that continues to shape beliefs, values, and societies worldwide. Spanning a period of approximately three years, his teachings, miracles, and interactions with people left an indelible impact on individuals, communities, and the course of human history.

Central to Jesus' ministry was his message of love, compassion, and forgiveness. He challenged societal norms and religious traditions of his time, advocating for a deeper understanding of God's kingdom based on humility, service, and inclusivity. This revolutionary approach to faith and spirituality resonated deeply with people from all walks of life, transcending social barriers and offering hope to the marginalized and oppressed.

Jesus' teachings, often conveyed through parables, addressed fundamental aspects of human existence: the nature of God's kingdom, the importance of faith and repentance, and the call to love one another as God loves us. His Sermon on the Mount, recorded in the Gospel of Matthew, encapsulates his ethical teachings, including the Beatitudes, which emphasize virtues such as meekness, mercy, and peacemaking.

Moreover, Jesus' ministry was characterized by miraculous healings, exorcisms, and demonstrations of divine power over nature. These acts not only validated his authority but also revealed God's compassion and desire to restore wholeness to individuals physically, spiritually, and emotionally afflicted.

Beyond his teachings and miracles, Jesus' personal interactions exemplified a profound empathy and concern for individuals. He engaged with outcasts, sinners, and those deemed unworthy by societal standards, demonstrating that God's love extends to all, regardless of their past or status.

The impact of Jesus' ministry extends beyond his immediate followers and continues to shape contemporary society in several profound ways. Christianity, founded on the teachings of Jesus Christ, has become one of the world's largest religions, influencing ethics, law, art, literature, and social institutions globally.

Ethically, Jesus' emphasis on love, justice, and compassion underpins many humanitarian efforts and social justice movements. The principles of caring for the poor, advocating for the oppressed, and promoting peace resonate deeply with Christian teachings derived from Jesus' ministry.

In conclusion, the impact of Jesus' ministry from the Gospels is profound and multifaceted. His teachings, miracles, and personal example continue to inspire billions of people worldwide to live lives of faith, love, and service. The enduring legacy of Jesus Christ's ministry underscores its relevance in addressing contemporary challenges and shaping a more compassionate and just world.

1. **Love and Compassion**: Jesus' central message was one of love and compassion. He demonstrated through his actions that genuine love extends to all people, irrespective of their background, status, or past. This inclusive love challenges us to treat others with kindness and empathy, fostering a sense of community and unity.

2. **Forgiveness and Grace**: Jesus emphasized the importance of forgiveness, both receiving and giving. His ministry showed that forgiveness leads to healing and reconciliation, offering individuals the opportunity to experience God's grace and transform their lives.

3. **Humility and Service**: Jesus taught by example the virtues of humility and service. He washed the feet of his disciples, illustrating that true leadership involves selflessness and a willingness to serve others. This model of servant leadership inspires individuals to prioritize the needs of others over personal gain.

4. **Faith and Repentance**: Throughout his ministry, Jesus called for faith in God and repentance from sin. He challenged people to turn away from wrongdoing and embrace a life of faithfulness to God's will. This emphasis on spiritual renewal continues to guide individuals in seeking a deeper relationship with God and striving for moral integrity.

5. **Inclusivity and Justice**: Jesus broke societal norms by welcoming marginalized groups, such as tax collectors, sinners, and the poor. He advocated for social justice and equality, emphasizing the dignity and worth of every human being. This call to uphold justice and dignity inspires efforts to address systemic injustices and promote human rights globally.

6. **Miracles and Divine Power**: Jesus' miracles demonstrated God's power and compassion. They affirmed his authority as the Son of God and offered hope to those suffering from physical, spiritual, and emotional afflictions. These miracles underscore the belief in God's ability to intervene in human affairs and bring about transformation.

7. **Legacy of Faith**: The enduring impact of Jesus' ministry is evident in Christianity's global influence. His teachings have shaped ethical principles, influenced legal systems, inspired artistic expression, and informed social movements. The legacy of faith and service continues to motivate individuals and communities to work towards a more just and compassionate world.

Conclusion

By integrating these biblical principles into their leadership practices, readers of "Divine Leadership" can cultivate environments of trust, growth, and innovation. These principles not only elevate individual leadership effectiveness but also contribute to broader societal and organizational transformation, aligning vision with purpose and inspiring others to reach their fullest potential.

Call to Action

1. **Vision and Purpose**: Leaders should cultivate a clear vision that aligns with their core values and mission, akin to Moses' vision to lead the Israelites out of Egypt and Nehemiah's determination to rebuild Jerusalem. This clarity empowers teams and organizations to pursue ambitious goals with unified effort and commitment.

2. **Integrity and Character**: Upholding unwavering integrity, as seen in Joseph's moral fortitude in Egypt and Daniel's steadfastness in the face of adversity, is foundational. Leaders must prioritize honesty, transparency, and ethical conduct to earn trust and credibility among their teams and stakeholders.

3. **Wisdom and Discernment**: Leaders should seek divine wisdom, exemplified by Solomon's request and Paul's discernment in ministry, to navigate complex decisions with insight and foresight. This practice ensures sound judgment and strategic direction in times of uncertainty.

4. **Faith and Courage**: Like David facing Goliath and Esther risking her life to save her people, leaders are called to exhibit faith and courage in confronting challenges. Encouraging teams to embrace bold initiatives and persevere through adversity fosters a culture of resilience and achievement.

5. **Resilience and Perseverance**: Drawing inspiration from Job's endurance and Paul's unwavering commitment, leaders should cultivate resilience and perseverance amidst setbacks. This resilience fuels innovation and adaptive strategies needed to thrive in dynamic environments.

6. **Servant Leadership**: Emulating Jesus' humility in serving others and Moses' delegation of responsibilities, leaders should adopt a servant leadership mindset. Prioritizing the needs and development of team members cultivates a supportive and empowered organizational culture.

7. **Communication and Collaboration**: Effective communication, exemplified by Nehemiah's strategic approach and Paul's collaborative efforts, is essential. Leaders must foster open dialogue and synergy among diverse teams to achieve collective objectives and overcome obstacles.

8. **Conflict Resolution and Unity**: Leaders should address conflicts with grace and wisdom, following Jesus' compassionate example and the Council of Jerusalem's resolution. Promoting reconciliation and unity strengthens team cohesion and enhances productivity.

9. **Mentorship and Succession Planning**: Investing in mentorship, modeled by Moses and Paul's guidance of successors, ensures continuity and growth within organizations. Developing future leaders nurtures a legacy of leadership excellence and organizational resilience.

10. **Leaving a Lasting Legacy**: Leaders are called to leave a lasting positive impact, mirroring King David's legacy and the profound influence of Jesus' ministry. Inspiring others through exemplary leadership and transformative actions ensures a enduring legacy of positive change.

Notes

www.ingramcontent.com/pod-product-compliance
Lightning Source LLC
Chambersburg PA
CBHW061730020426

42331CB00006B/1182